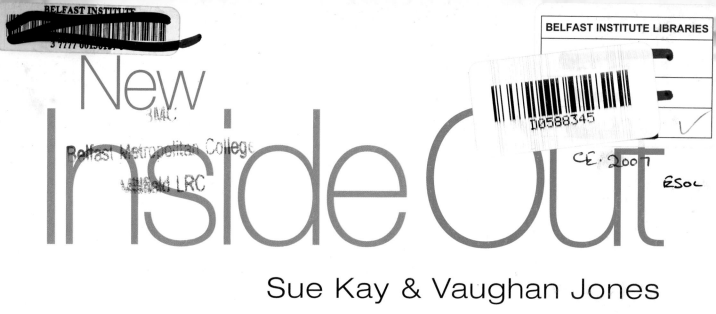

New Inside Out

Sue Kay & Vaughan Jones

with Peter Maggs & Catherine Smith

Bell

·Beginner

Student's Book

MACMILLAN

WB = **Workbook**. Each unit of the Workbook contains a one-page section which develops practical writing skills.

0 Instructions

1 🔊 1.01 **Listen and repeat the instructions.**

2 🌐 1.02 **Listen and repeat the instructions.**

> How are you?

> I'm fine, thanks.

a) Look at the photos. b) Listen and repeat. c) Practise the conversation.

d) Read the text. e) Compare your sentences. f) Check your answers.

3 🌐 1.03 **Read and listen to the instructions.**

a) **Complete.** Hello. My name's Mario.

b) (**Circle**). Hello. My name's (Mario).

c) <u>**Underline.**</u> Hello. My name's <u>Mario</u>.

d) **Tick (✔)** 1 ☐ 2 ☐ 3 ✔ 4 ☐

e) **Cross out.** Hello. My name's M̶a̶r̶i̶o̶.

f) **Match.** 1 France

2 Brazil

3 Japan

4 **Follow the instructions.**

1 **Complete the sentence.** Hello. My name's _____ .

2 (**Circle**) **the name.** Hello. My name's Tina.

3 <u>**Underline**</u> *Hello*. Hello. My name's Karl.

4 **Tick (✓) the correct box.** I'm a man (♂). ☐ I'm a woman (♀). ☐

5 **Cross out the incorrect word.** Inglish English.

6 **Match the numbers.** 1   two

2   three

3   one

1 ID

Grammar *my/your/his/her*. Singular and plural nouns. *this/these*
Vocabulary Names. Numbers *1–10*. Common objects
Useful phrases Personal information

Grammar

Possessive determiners

my name
your name

***be*: contractions**

I**'m** = I **am**
My name**'s** = My name **is**
What**'s** = What **is**

1　🌐 **1.04 Listen and complete.**
'What's your name?'
'My name's Bond ... _____ Bond.'

2　🌐 **1.05 Listen and complete with**
***my* or *your*.**
'Hello. I'm Jinx. What's _____ name?'
'_____ name's Bond ... James Bond.'
'Nice to meet you, James.'

Practise the conversation with a partner.

Speaking

Speak to other students. Practise the conversation with your names.

> Hello. I'm Manolo. What's your name?

> My name's Ana Ramirez.

> Nice to meet you, Ana.

Grammar

Pierce Brosnan and Teri Hatcher in *Tomorrow Never Dies* – 1997

Possessive determiners

his name
her name

1 🌐 1.06 **Listen and complete with** *his* (♂) **or** *her* (♀).

a) 'What's _____ name?' '_____ name's Pierce Brosnan.'

b) 'What's _____ name?' '_____ name's Teri Hatcher.'

2 **Ask questions about students in your class.**

What's his name?

Rafael.

What's her name?

Magda.

Vocabulary

Numbers

0 = <u>zero</u> / oh
1 = one
2 = two
3 = three
4 = four
5 = five
6 = six
7 = <u>seven</u>
8 = eight
9 = nine
10 = ten

007 = <u>double</u> oh, <u>seven</u>

1 🌐 1.07 **Listen and repeat the numbers.**

2 **Complete the lists.**

a) one two *three* _____ _____

b) five four _____ _____ _____

c) two four _____ _____ _____

d) one three five _____ _____

🌐 1.08 **Listen, check and repeat.**

3 🌐 1.09 **Listen and write the phone numbers.**

a) 'What's your home (🏠) number?' '*020* _____ _____ .'

b) 'What's your mobile (📱) number?' '_____ _____ _____ .'

Speaking

Names

first name = James
<u>surname</u> = Bond

Ask two students. Complete the information.

What's your first name?

Luigi.

What's your surname?

Alongi.

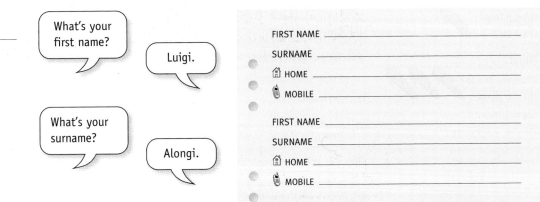

FIRST NAME _____

SURNAME _____

🏠 HOME _____

📱 MOBILE _____

FIRST NAME _____

SURNAME _____

🏠 HOME _____

📱 MOBILE _____

Vocabulary

1 🌐 **1.10 Listen and repeat the words.**

1	a bag	4	pens	7	a <u>pass</u>port
2	a com<u>pu</u>ter	5	keys	8	a <u>ca</u>mera
3	books	6	a <u>mo</u>bile <u>phone</u>		

2 Cover the words. Say a number. Your partner says the word.

Two.

A computer.

Four.

Pens.

Grammar

 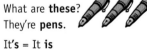

Nouns; *this/these*

Singular

What's **this**?
It's **a pen**.

Plural

What are **these**?
They're **pens**.

It'**s** = It **is**
They'**re** = They **are**

1 Look at the photo above. <u>Underline</u> the correct answer.

1	'What's this?'	'<u>It's a bag.</u> / They're bags.'
2	'What's this?'	'It's a computer. / They're computers.'
3	'What are these?'	'It's a book. / They're books.'
4	'What are these?'	'It's a pen. / They're pens.'
5	'What are these?'	'It's a key. / They're keys.'
6	'What's this?'	'It's a mobile phone. / They're mobile phones.'
7	'What's this?'	'It's a passport. / They're passports.'
8	'What's this?'	'It's a camera. / They're cameras.'

🌐 **1.11 Listen, check and repeat.**

2 Grammar *Extra* **1** page 126. Read the explanation and do the exercises.

Listening

1 🔘 1.12 **Listen to the conversation. Tick (✓) the things in her bag. Tick (✓) the things in his bag.**

Her bag	Things	His bag
✓	a computer	___
___	a camera	___
___	books	___
___	a mobile phone	___
___	a passport	___

2 What *isn't* in his bag?

Pronunciation

The alphabet

A B	C D	E F	G
H I	J K	L M N O	P
Q R	S	T U	V
W	X	Y	Z

1 🔘 1.13 **Listen and repeat the letters.**

2 🔘 1.14 **Listen and complete with the letters in the box.**

A ~~E~~ I O U

1   /iː/   B C D E G P T V
2   /e/   F L M N S X Z
3   /eɪ/   __ H J K
4   /uː/   Q __ W
5   /aɪ/   __ Y
6   /əʊ/   __
7   /ɑː/   R

Repeat the letters.

3 🔘 1.15 **Listen and number (1–6) the abbreviations as you hear them.**

OK ☐   CIA ☐   VIP ☐   NYC ☐   UK ☐   USA 1

Repeat the abbreviations.

Useful phrases

1 🌐 **1.16 Read, listen and complete the conversation.**

Receptionist: Welcome to The London English School.
               What's your name?
Student: Tusanee.
Receptionist: Can you spell that, please?
Student: T–U–S–A–N–E–E.
Receptionist: And your surname?
Student: (1) *R–0–0* _____ .
Receptionist: Sorry, can you repeat that, please?
Student: (2) _____ .
Receptionist: Thank you, Miss (3) _____ .
Student: Please call me Nut.
Receptionist: OK. Thank you, Nut.

Listen and check.

2 🌐 **1.17 Listen and repeat the useful phrases.**

a) Can you spell that, please?
b) Sorry, can you repeat that, please?
c) Please call me Nut.

3 Work with a partner. Write a new conversation about one of these students.

Practise the conversation.

4 Pairwork **Student A:** page 116 **Student B:** page 121

Vocabulary *Extra*

Everyday objects

1 Match the pictures with the words.

- `6` a bag
- ☐ a book
- ☐ a camera
- ☐ a computer
- ☐ a dictionary
- ☐ a key
- ☐ a mobile phone
- ☐ a passport
- ☐ a pen

2 Work with a partner. Cover the words. Look at the pictures. Ask and answer questions.

> What's this?

> It's a mobile phone.

Numbers

1 Match the numbers (*1–10*) with the words in the box.

eight	five	four	nine	~~one~~
<u>seven</u>	six	ten	three	two

1 *one*   6 ____
2 ____   7 ____
3 ____   8 ____
4 ____   9 ____
5 ____   10 ____

2 Dictate three numbers to your partner.

> 4

> 6

> 10

four   six   ten

Check your partner's numbers.

2 International

Grammar *be*: present simple. Prepositions: *in/near. How much ...?*
Vocabulary Countries. Nationalities. Numbers *11–100*. Prices
Useful phrases In a shop.

Vocabulary

1 🌐 1.18 Listen to the introductions in *International Pop Star* and complete the table.

| Brazil | Germany | ~~Italy~~ | Japan | Poland | Spain |

☐ ☐ ☐	☐ ☐	☐ ☐	☐
1 *Italy*	3 _____	4 _____	6 _____
2 _____		5 _____	

2 🌐 1.19 Listen and repeat the countries.

What's the name of your country in English?

Grammar

be

I'm — I am
You're — You are
He's — He is
She's — She is
It's — It is
We're — We are
They're — They are

Is Ken from Poland?
Yes, he is.
No, he isn't.
(isn't = is not)

1 Complete the questions and answers with *I, you, he, she, we* or *they.*

a) 'Is Anna from Germany?' 'Yes, *she* is.' 'No, *she* isn't.'
b) 'Is Rosa from Japan?' 'Yes, _____ is.' 'No, _____ isn't.'
c) 'Is Daniel from Poland?' 'Yes, _____ is.' 'No, _____ isn't.'
d) 'Are Roberto and Donna from Brazil?' 'Yes, _____ are.' 'No, _____ aren't.'
e) 'Are you from Spain?' 'Yes, _____ am.' 'No, _____ 'm not.'
f) 'Are you and your teacher from Italy?' 'Yes, _____ are.' 'No, _____ aren't.'

🌐 1.20 Listen, check and repeat.

2 Work with a partner. Ask and answer the questions in Exercise 1.

3 Pairwork Student A: page 116 Student B: page 121

4 Grammar *Extra* 2 page 126. Read the explanation and do the exercises.

Grammar

Prepositions

in

near

1 🔘 **1.21 Listen and <u>underline</u> the correct answers.**

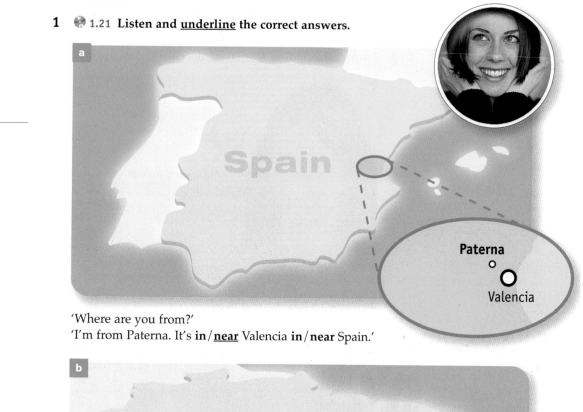

a

Spain

Paterna
○
O
Valencia

'Where are you from?'
'I'm from Paterna. It's **in**/<u>**near**</u> Valencia **in**/**near** Spain.'

b

Brazil

Rio de Janeiro
O ○
Niteroi

'Where are you from?'
'We're from Niteroi. It's **in**/**near** Rio de Janeiro **in**/**near** Brazil.'
Practise the questions and answers.

2 **Complete the sentence.**
I'm from _____ . It's (near _____) in _____ .

Speaking

1 **Ask three students.**

> Where are
> you from?

> I'm from Katowice. It's
> near Krakow in Poland.

2 **Ask questions about students in your class.**

> Where is
> Mario from?

> He's from
> Bologna.

> Is Eli from
> Bologna?

> No, she isn't.
> She's from Modena.

Vocabulary (1)

Nationalities

🟦 American

🔵 Brazilian

🇬🇧 British

⬛ German

🟩 Italian

⚪ Japanese

⬜ Polish

🟥 Spanish

1 🌐 1.22 Listen and repeat the nationalities.

2 Look at the photos. <u>Underline</u> the correct description.

a) She's <u>**Spanish**</u> / **Brazilian**.
b) It's **German** / **Polish**.
c) He's **American** / **British**.

d) They're **Italian** / **Spanish**.
e) They're **American** / **Japanese**.
f) They're **German** / **Italian**.

🌐 1.23 Listen, check and repeat.

Vocabulary (2)

Numbers

11 = eleven
12 = twelve
13 = thirteen
14 = fourteen
15 = fifteen
16 = sixteen
17 = seventeen
18 = eighteen
19 = nineteen

20 = twenty
30 = thirty
40 = forty
50 = fifty
60 = sixty
70 = seventy
80 = eighty
90 = ninety

100 = one hundred

1 🌐 1.24 Listen and repeat the numbers.

2 Say the numbers 1–20 with a partner.

3 Complete each line.
   a) 21 = twenty-one   22 = twenty-two   23 = *twenty-three*
   b) 34 = thirty-four   35 = thirty-five   36 = _____
   c) 47 = forty-seven   48 = forty-eight   49 = _____
   d) 111 = one hundred and eleven   112 = one hundred and twelve   113 = _____

   🌐 1.25 Listen and check.

4 🌐 1.26 Listen and join the numbers.

a)
○ 13   ○ 30   ○ 74
○ 59   ○ 66   ○ 81
○ 98   ○ 14   ○ 40

b)
○ 15   ○ 24   ○ 119
○ 50   ○ 83   ○ 190
○ 99   ○ 199   ○ 7

c)
○ 18   ○ 17   ○ 29
○ 70   ○ 80   ○ 38
○ 79   ○ 116   ○ 160

What's the mystery number?

5 Say a number from 1–199. Your partner says the next three numbers.

Sixty-four.   Sixty-five, sixty-six, sixty-seven.

Pronunciation

1 Match the words with the signs.

a) euros   £
b) dollars   €
c) pounds $

🌐 **1.27** Listen and repeat the words.

2 🌐 **1.28** Circle the price you hear.

a) ($3.50) $3.15
b) £5.30   £5.13
c) €17.75   €70.75
d) $90.99 $19.99
e) €18.20   €80.20
f) €40.40   €14.40
g) £160.00   £116.00

Listen again and repeat the prices.

Listening

1 🌐 **1.29** Listen and complete the table with the missing prices.

		a cappuccino	a hamburger	a cinema ticket	a night in a 3-star hotel
1	New York	a) *$3.00*	$3.00	$9.00	$200.00
2	Moscow	$2.50	b) _____	$5.00	$90.00
3	Rome	$1.25	$3.75	$8.85	$100.00
4	London	$3.40	$3.60	c) _____	$129.00
5	Tokyo	$3.20	$2.50	$16.50	d) _____
6	_____	_____	_____	_____	_____

(The prices are in US dollars.)

2 Work with a partner. Complete row 6 in the table with the prices in your city.

Grammar

How much ...?

How much is a cappuccino in Moscow?

1 Put the words in the correct order.

a) in Rome? / is / a cappuccino / How much   *How much is a cappuccino in Rome?*
b) How much / in London? / a hamburger / is
c) is / a cinema ticket / How much / in Tokyo?
d) a 3-star hotel / in Moscow? / is / How much

🌐 **1.30** Listen, check and repeat the questions.

2 Work with a partner. Ask and answer the questions in Exercise 1.

3 Look at the table in Listening Exercise 1 and ask your partner more questions.

> How much is a cinema ticket in New York?

> Nine dollars.

> How much is a cappuccino in (your city)?

Useful phrases

1 Complete the conversations with the words in the box.

are	is	these	this

a

'How much is _____ ?'
'Twelve dollars fifty.'
'OK, thanks.'

b

'How much are _____ ?'
'Nine euros.'
'OK, thanks.'

c

'How much _____ this?'
'Six euros twenty.'
'OK, thanks.'

d

'How much _____ these?'
'One hundred and seventy-five euros.'
'Oh! OK, no thanks.'

🌐 1.31 **Listen and check.**

2 🌐 1.32 **Listen and repeat the useful phrases.**

a) How much is this?
b) How much are these?

3 Work with a partner. Practise the conversations.

Vocabulary *Extra*

Countries and nationalities

Look at the photos. For each photo write
a) the country and b) the nationality.
Use the words in the box.

American	Spain	Italian	~~Poland~~
Japanese	Brazil	Japan	German
the UK	the USA	Brazilian	Germany
~~Polish~~	Italy	British	Spanish

Numbers

1 Match the numbers with the words in the box.

eighteen	eighty	~~eleven~~	fifteen
fifty	forty	fourteen	nineteen
ninety	one hundred	seventeen	
seventy	sixteen	sixty	thirteen
thirty	twelve	twenty	

11 *eleven*
12 _____
13 _____
14 _____
15 _____
16 _____
17 _____
18 _____
19 _____
20 _____
30 _____
40 _____
50 _____
60 _____
70 _____
80 _____
90 _____
100 _____

2 Dictate three numbers to your partner.

(19) (50) (100)

nineteen   fifty   one hundred

Check your partner's numbers.

Warsaw
a) *Poland*
b) *Polish*

Berlin
a) _____
b) _____

Madrid
a) _____
b) _____

New York
a) _____
b) _____

Pisa
a) _____
b) _____

Kyoto
a) _____
b) _____

Rio de Janeiro
a) _____
b) _____

London
a) _____
b) _____

3 Relations

Grammar *How old ...?* Possessive *'s. our/their. have/has*
Vocabulary Family
Useful phrases Introductions

Listening

My family.

My mum. My dad. My brother. Me. My sister. Grandma. Grandpa. My dog.
Helen   William   Sam   Luisa Emma   Hannah   Tom   Max

1 🌐 **1.33 Listen to Luisa and match the family words with the names.**

1 mother (mum)
2 father (dad)
3 brother
4 sister
5 grandmother (grandma)
6 grandfather (grandpa)

Emma
Tom
William
Hannah
Helen
Sam

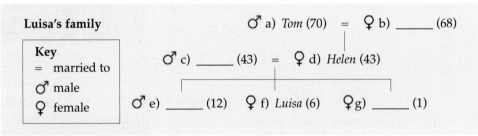

2 🌐 **1.34 Listen and repeat the family words.**

▲ Luisa

3 Complete the family tree.

Luisa's family		♂ a) *Tom* (70) = ♀ b) _____ (68)
Key = married to ♂ male ♀ female	♂ c) _____ (43) = ♀ d) *Helen* (43)	
	♂ e) _____ (12) ♀ f) *Luisa* (6) ♀ g) _____ (1)	

Grammar

How old ...?

How old are you?
I'm 24.

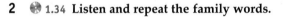

1 🌐 **1.35 Listen to Luisa and complete the questions and answers.**

a) 'How old *are* you?'   '*I'm* six.'
b) 'How old *is* your brother?'   '*He's* twelve.'
c) 'How old _____ your sister?'   '_____ one.'
d) 'How old _____ your mother and father?'   '_____ forty-three.'
e) 'How old _____ your grandmother?'   '_____ sixty-eight.'
f) 'How old _____ your grandfather?'   '_____ seventy.'

2 Work with a partner. Ask and answer the questions in Exercise 1.

Grammar

Possessive 's / s'

My brother**'s** name is Sam.
(brother**'s** is singular)

My sister**s'** names are Luisa
and Emma.
(sister**s'** is plural)

1 **Complete the sentences.**

a) Helen is Luisa's *mother*.

b) Sam is Luisa's _____ .

c) Tom is Luisa's _____ .

d) Emma is Luisa's _____ .

e) William is Luisa's _____ .

f) Hannah is Luisa's _____ .

🌐 1.36 **Listen, check and repeat.**

2 **Match the descriptions (*a–c*) with the names, *Emma, Helen* and *Sam*.**

a) His father's name is William, and his sisters' names are Luisa and Emma. Who is he?

b) Her brother's name is Sam, and her sister's name is Luisa. Who is she?

c) Her father's name is Tom, and her mother's name is Hannah. Who is she?

Listening

1 🌐 1.37 **Listen to Tom. Put the family photos (*a–c*) in the correct order (*1–3*).**

Helen and William   Hannah and Tom   Sam, Luisa and Emma

2 **Listen again. Underline the correct word.**

a) Hannah is Tom's **husband** / **wife**.

b) Helen is Tom's **son** / **daughter**.

c) Sam is Tom's **grandson** / **granddaughter**.

Vocabulary

1 🌐 1.38 **Listen and repeat the family words.**

Family						
♀	mother	daughter	grandmother	granddaughter	sister	wife
♂	father	son	grandfather	grandson	brother	husband
♀ + ♂	parents	children	grandparents	grandchildren		

2 **Write six more sentences about Tom and Luisa's family relations.**

1 Tom is Hannah's husband.
2 Helen and William are Luisa's parents.

3 **Who are you? Write six sentences.**

1 I'm Olga's son.
2 I'm Natasha's brother.

3 I'm Dimitri's grandson.
4 ...

Compare with a partner.

4 Pairwork **Student A:** page 116   **Student B:** page 121

Reading

1 🌐 1.39 **Read and match the texts (*a* and *b*) with the photos (*1* and *2*).**

a) This is John Travolta's house in Florida, USA. He has six cars and two planes. John's wife, Kelly Preston, is an actor, and they have two children. Their son's name is Jett, and their daughter's name is Ella Bleu.

b) Blythe Danner is an American actor. She has two children and they're also actors. Her daughter is Gwyneth Paltrow, and her son is Jake Paltrow. She has a granddaughter and a grandson. Their names are Apple Blythe Alison Martin and Moses Martin.

2 **Who says it? Match the sentences (*a–d*) with the correct names (*1–4*).**

a) 'My mother is an actor. Her name is Blythe Danner.'
b) 'My children are actors. Their names are Gwyneth and Jake.'
c) 'Our son's name is Jett and our daughter's name is Ella Bleu.'
d) 'We live in Florida. Our dad has six cars and two planes.'

1 Jett and Ella Bleu Travolta
2 Gwyneth Paltrow
3 Blythe Danner
4 John Travolta and Kelly Preston

Grammar

Possessive determiners

I ➔ **my** mother

you ➔ **your** father

he ➔ **his** sister

she ➔ **her** brother

we ➔ **our** children

they ➔ **their** parents

1 **Complete the sentences with *my*, *his*, *her*, *our* or *their*.**

a) John Travolta and *his* wife are American.

b) Blythe Danner and _____ children are actors.

c) Jake Paltrow and _____ sister are actors.

d) John Travolta, Kelly Preston and _____ two children live in Florida.

e) Jett Travolta says, '_____ sister and I are American. _____ parents are from the USA.'

🌐 1.40 **Listen, check and repeat.**

2 Grammar *Extra* 3 page 126. Read the explanation and do the exercises.

Grammar

have

I **have**
You **have**
He **has**
She **has**
It **has**
We **have**
They **have**

1 <u>Underline</u> the correct form.

a) I **has** / **have** one sister and
one brother.

b) My parents **has** / **have**
a dog.

c) My mother **has** / **have**
three brothers.

d) My grandparents **has** / **have**
two houses.

e) My husband and I **has** / **have**
two children.

f) My father **has** / **have**
a Japanese car.

🔘 1.41 **Listen, check and repeat.**

2 Which sentences are true for you?

Pronunciation

1 🌐 1.42 **Listen and repeat.**

a) He's a teacher. She's an‿actor.

b) He has a radio. She has an‿iPod.

c) He has a Fiat. She has an‿Alfa Romeo.

2 Complete the table with the nouns in the box.

| Audi | brother | dog | English dictionary | Ericsson mobile phone |
| Gucci bag | IBM computer | Italian grandmother | passport | sister |

an + vowel sound	*a* + consonant sound
an Audi	*a brother*

🌐 1.43 **Listen, check and repeat.**

3 Tell your partner about things you have. Use *a* or *an*.

I have a dog.   I have an iPod.

Writing

1 Write a paragraph about someone in your family.

Lourdes is my grandmother. She's my
mother's mother. She's seventy-three.
She's from Vega de Pas near Santander
in Spain. She has four children and seven
grandchildren. Her husband's name is Juan.

2 Compare with a partner.

Useful phrases

1 🌐 1.44 **Read and listen to the conversations. Answer the questions.**

a) Who's Ann's brother?
b) Who's Becky's husband?

Ann Tim Gerry Rob Becky Julia

Tim: This is Ann. She's my sister.
Gerry: Nice to meet you. I'm Gerry.
Ann: Nice to meet you.

Rob: This is Julia. She's Brazilian.
Becky: Nice to meet you. I'm Rob's wife.
Julia: Nice to meet you.

2 🌐 1.45 **Listen and repeat the useful phrases.**

a) This is Ann.
b) Nice to meet you.
c) I'm Gerry.

3 **Complete the conversation with the words in the box.**

'm   meet   Nice   ~~This~~   to   you

Ann: (1) *This* is Tim.
Julia: (2) _____ to (3) _____ you. I (4) _____ Julia.
Tim: Nice (5) _____ meet (6) _____ .

🌐 1.46 **Listen and check.**

4 **Work in groups of three. Rewrite the conversation with *your* names.**

Practise the conversation.

Vocabulary *Extra*

Family

1 Complete the sentences with the words in the box.

brother   granddaughter
grandfather   ~~husband~~
mother   parents

Alice is Bill's wife.
Bill is Alice's *husband*.

Charlie is Alice and Bill's son.
Alice and Bill are Charlie's _____ .

Alice is Delia's grandmother.
Delia is Alice's _____ .

Delia is Ed's sister.
Ed is Delia's _____ .

Ed is Fran's son.
Fran is Ed's _____ .

Gary is Charlie's grandson.
Charlie is Gary's _____ .

2 Look at the family tree and answer the questions.

a)   Who is Delia's father?
b)   Who is Fran's daughter?
c)   Who is Charlie's wife?
d)   Who is Fran's grandson?
e)   Who are Ed's grandparents?
f)   Who is Gary's grandmother?

3 Write sentences about your family.

Greta is my wife. Rosa is my …

Family tree

Alice = Bill

|

Charlie = Fran

Delia   Ed

|

Gary

Review A

Grammar

► Grammar *Extra* pages 126 and 127

1 Put the words in the correct order.

a) your / What's / name / mother's ?
What's your mother's name ?
b) is / How / she / old ?
c) is / Where / she / from ?
d) her / What's / nationality ?
e) number / What's / phone / her ?
f) is / Where / now / she ?

Answer the questions. Write sentences.

a) *My mother's name is Ana.*

2 Write questions and answers.

a) *What's this? It's a car.*
b) *What are these? ...*

3 Choose a word in the box to describe each object in Exercise 2.

| American English German Japanese Polish |

a) *It's German.*

4 Complete the sentences with *my, your, his, her, our* or *their*.

William   Harry   Anne   Andrew   Edward

Elizabeth   Philip   Charles   Camilla

a) My name's Charles. This is *my* family.
b) We're English. _____ surname's Windsor.
c) This is my wife. _____ name's Camilla.
d) These are my sons. _____ names are William and Harry.
e) This is my father. _____ name's Philip.
f) You're an English student. What's _____ name?

5 Complete the sentences about Prince Charles.

a) His *wife's* name is Camilla.
b) His _____ name is Elizabeth.
c) His _____ name is Philip.
d) His _____ names are William and Harry.
e) His _____ name is Anne.
f) His _____ names are Andrew and Edward.

6 Spot the mistake! Cross out the incorrect sentence, *a* or *b*.

1 a) ~~My name Tom.~~
   b) My name's Tom.
2 a) What is?
   b) What's this?
3 a) Where Mario from?
   b) Where's Mario from?
4 a) They're from Spain.
   b) They're from in Spain.
5 a) I'm twenty.
   b) I have twenty years.
6 a) She has two children.
   b) She have two children.

Vocabulary

1 Complete the instructions with the verbs in the box.

> Ask   ~~Listen~~   Look   Match   Practise   Work

a) *Listen* and repeat.
b) _____ the conversation.
c) _____ your partner.
d) _____ at the photos.
e) _____ the pictures with the words.
f) _____ with a partner.

2 Complete the crossword with the numbers one to ten.

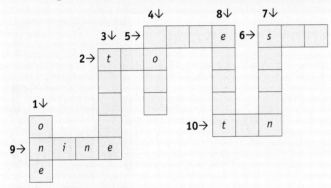

3 Complete the sentences.

a) Rome is the capital of *Italy*.
b) Tokyo is the capital of _____ .
c) Madrid is the capital of _____ .
d) Warsaw is the capital of _____ .
e) Brasilia is the capital of _____ .
f) Berlin is the capital of _____ .

4 Write the prices.

a) $12.55 *Twelve dollars fifty-five*
b) £24.99
c) €15.75
d) €37.80
e) $69.19
f) $149.50

5 Complete the word puzzle.

1   son and …
2   mother and …
3   father and …

4   wife and …
5   husband and …
6   grandfather and …

7   brother and …
8   sister and …
9   daughter and …
10   granddaughter and …

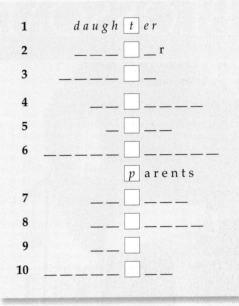

What's the name of the famous family?

Pronunciation

1 Look at some words from Units 1–3. Say the words and add them to the table.

> ~~adjective~~   ~~computer~~   description
> Germany   granddaughter   ~~Japanese~~
> possessive   relation   seventeen   singular

A: ☐☐☐	B: ☐☐☐	C: ☐☐☐
adjective	*computer*	*Japanese*

2 <u>Underline</u> the stressed syllable in each word.

🔊 1.47 **Listen, check and repeat.**

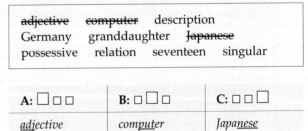

1 Read the information about Blossoms Hotel. Are the sentences true or false?

a) Blossoms Hotel is in London.
b) It's near the train station.
c) It has nineteen rooms.
d) A room for one night is 85 euros.
e) The hotel has a fish restaurant.

WELCOME TO

BLOSSOMS HOTEL

SITUATED IN THE HISTORIC

CITY OF BATH

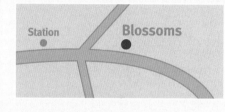

Station   Blossoms

Near train station, museums, galleries and shops
Nine rooms
Price: one night = £85
Fish restaurant

Station Street
Bath BA1 1EF
telephone +44(0)1225 420 350
www.blossomshotelbath.co.uk

2 🌐 1.48 **Listen to the conversation. Underline the correct information.**

a) The man books: (1) one night (2) two nights (3) three nights.

b) He's: (1) German (2) American (3) English.

c) His room number is: (1) 101 (2) 102 (3) 103.

3 Listen again and complete the information on the form.

BLOSSOMS

HOTEL

FIRST NAME:	A _ n _ l _
SURNAME:	S _ h w a _ z e _ e _ g _ r
NATIONALITY:	_ _ _ _ _ _ _
CITY:	Los Angeles
COUNTRY:	USA
PHONE NUMBER:	001-31 _ -8 _ 3-4 _ 9
PASSPORT NUMBER:	489- _ _ _ -2340

Writing & Speaking

1 Complete the rules for capital letters. Use examples from the Blossoms Hotel form below.

You use capital letters for …

a) first names: *Susan*

b) surnames: _____

c) nationalities: _____

d) street names: _____

e) cities: _____

f) countries: _____

FIRST NAME:	Susan
SURNAME:	Barclay
NATIONALITY:	British
ADDRESS:	14 Wellington Street
CITY:	Glasgow
COUNTRY:	Scotland
PHONE NUMBER:	0141-333-622
EMAIL ADDRESS:	susan@barclay.co.uk
PASSPORT NUMBER:	307612377
DATE:	30/06/07
SIGNATURE:	Susan Barclay

2 Match the questions (*a–g*) with the information (*1–7*) in the form below.

a) What's your nationality? 3

b) What's your surname?

c) What's your phone number?

d) What's your address?

e) What's your email address?

f) What's your first name?

g) What's your passport number?

1	FIRST NAME:	_____
2	SURNAME:	_____
3	NATIONALITY:	_____
4	ADDRESS:	_____
	CITY:	_____
	COUNTRY:	_____
5	PHONE NUMBER:	_____
6	EMAIL ADDRESS:	_____
7	PASSPORT NUMBER:	_____
	DATE:	_____
	SIGNATURE:	_____

Ask your partner the questions.

Complete the form with their information.

4 Favourites

Grammar *like / don't like.* Adjective + noun word order
Vocabulary Food. Drink. Sport. Colours. Adjectives
Useful phrases Asking for clarification

Vocabulary

1 Complete the table below.

fruit ▶

▲ Coke   ▲ swimming   ▲ wine   ▲ coffee

▲ tennis   ▲ tea   ▲ football

▲ meat   ▲ fish   ▲ Italian food

▲ Chinese food

Food	Drink	Sport
fruit	Coke	*swimming*
meat	wine	___
___	___	
___		

🌐 1.49 **Listen, check and repeat.**

2 Say a word. Your partner says which list.

meat   food

Grammar

like

I **like** pasta. ☺
I **don't like** pizza. ☹
(don**'t** = do **not**)

Do you **like** pasta?
Yes, I **do**. ☺
No, I **don't**. ☹

1 🌐 1.50 **Listen and repeat the conversation.**

Ann: Do you like pasta?
Beth: No, I don't.
Ann: Do you like pizza?
Beth: No, I don't.
Ann: Do you like Italian food?
Beth: No, I like Chinese food.
Ann: But this is an Italian restaurant!
Beth: Oh!

Practise with a partner.

2 **Complete the questions and answers.**

a) '*Do* you like Italian food?'   'Yes, I *do*.'   'No, I *don't*.'

b) '_____ you like Chinese food?' 'Yes, I _____ .' 'No, I _____ .'

c) '_____ you _____ fish?' 'Yes, I _____ .' 'No, I _____ .'

d) '_____ fruit?' 'Yes, _____ .' 'No, _____ .'

e) '_____ coffee?' 'Yes, _____ .' 'No, _____ .'

f) '_____ Coke?' 'Yes, _____ .' 'No, _____ .'

🌐 1.51 **Listen, check and repeat.**

3 **Work with a partner. Ask and answer the questions in Exercise 2.**

Ask six more questions.

> Do you like Johnny Depp?

> Yes, I do!

Reading & Writing

1 🌐 1.52 **Read the web profile.**

> **PROFILE Nina Frank**
> **Job:** Model   **Nationality:** South African
> a) **Favourite city:** Cape Town
> b) **Favourite actor:** George Clooney
> c) **Favourite singer:** Shakira
> d) **Favourite sport:** Swimming
> e) **Favourite food:** Pizza
> f) **Favourite drink:** Malibu and Coke

2 **Write questions about Nina's favourite things with *What* or *Who*.**

a) *What's her favourite city?*   b) *Who's her favourite actor?*

🌐 1.53 **Listen, check and repeat.**

3 **Work with a partner. Ask and answer the questions in Exercise 2.**

4 **Change the questions in Exercise 2 from *her* to *your* and ask your partner.**

> What's your favourite food?

> Spaghetti.

Write a web profile for your partner.

Vocabulary (1)

Colours

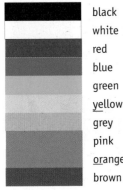

black
white
red
blue
green
<u>ye</u>llow
grey
pink
<u>or</u>ange
brown

1 🌐 1.54 Listen and repeat the colours.

What's your favourite colour?

1	2	**3**
	4	5
6	7	**8**
	9	**10**

2 Say a number. Your partner says which colour.

> Five.

> Green.

3 Ask your partner 'maths' questions.

> What's **black**, blue and **red**?

> Eight. (**1** + **4** + **3** = **8**)

Vocabulary (2)

1 Match the descriptions (*a–d*) with the photos (*1–4*).

a) A red bus, black taxis and expensive shops in London.
b) A big square with old buildings in Moscow.
c) Blue sky and beautiful people in Rio de Janeiro.
d) Small houses. Red, orange, blue and yellow walls in Buenos Aires.

1 Red Square

2 La Boca

3 Oxford Street

4 Copacabana Beach

🌐 1.55 Listen and check.

2 Match the adjectives in *A* with their opposites in *B*.

A	B
<u>beau</u>tiful	ex<u>pen</u>sive
big	old
cheap	<u>ug</u>ly
new	small

🌐 1.56 Listen, check and repeat.

3 ▮ Pairwork **Student A:** page 117 **Student B:** page 122

Pronunciation

1 🌐 **1.57 Listen and repeat.**

a) <u>Ve</u>nice <u>Mu</u>nich (Beijing)

b) Rome Florence Moscow

c) Seville Berlin Warsaw

d) Madrid London Paris

e) Russia France China

f) Cairo Tokyo Milan

2 Listen again and <u>underline</u> the stressed syllable.

Circle the city or country with a different stress in each group.

3 Ask your partner questions.

Where's Beijing?

It's in China.

Grammar

Adjective + noun word order

a red bus
NOT ~~a bus red~~
black taxis
NOT ~~blacks taxis~~

1 Put the words in the correct order.

a) coffee / black / like / I   *I like black coffee.*

b) I / French / like / films

c) old / I / buildings / like

d) expensive / like / I / shops

e) I / British / like / don't / food

f) big / like / I / cities / don't

🌐 **1.58 Listen, check and repeat.**

2 Make the sentences true for you.

I don't like black coffee. OR *I like white coffee.*

3 Combine adjectives and nouns. Write two lists.

Adjectives
American beautiful big black cheap expensive French new old red

Nouns
buildings cars cities coffee films food music restaurants shops wine

I like …	I don't like …
expensive restaurants *old buildings*	*American cars* *French music*

4 Grammar *Extra* 4 page 128. Read the explanation and do the exercises.

Speaking

Ask your partner questions.

Do you like expensive restaurants?

Yes, I do.

Do you like old buildings?

No, I don't.

Useful phrases

1 🌐 1.59 **Read, listen and complete the conversation with** *help*, *speak* **or** *understand*.

Waiter:	Can I (1) _____ you?
Customer:	Yes, please. What is 'cod'?
Waiter:	It's a kind of fish.
Customer:	I'm sorry. I don't (2) _____ .
Waiter:	IT'S A KIND OF FISH.
Customer:	Can you (3) _____ more slowly, please?
Waiter:	IT'S – A – KIND – OF – FISH.
Customer:	Oh, OK. One hamburger, please.

Listen and check.

2 **Complete the conversation.**

Waiter:	(1) _____ I (2) _____ you?
Customer:	Yes, please. What are 'lychees'?
Waiter:	They are a kind of fruit.
Customer:	I'm sorry. (3) _____ _____ _____ .
Waiter:	THEY'RE A KIND OF FRUIT.
Customer:	(4) _____ you (5) _____ more slowly, please?
Waiter:	THEY'RE – A – KIND – OF – FRUIT.
Customer:	Oh, OK. Ice cream, please.

🌐 1.60 **Listen, check and repeat.**

3 🌐 1.61 **Listen and repeat the useful phrases.**

a) Can I help you?
b) What are 'lychees'?
c) I'm sorry, I don't understand.
d) Can you speak more slowly, please?

4 **Work with a partner. Practise the conversations.**

MENU

Main dishes
cod and chips
hamburger
pizza

Desserts
apple pie
ice cream
lychees

Vocabulary *Extra*

Food and drink

1 Match the pictures with the words.

- [2] <u>cof</u>fee
- [ ] fish
- [ ] fruit
- [ ] meat
- [ ] <u>pas</u>ta
- [ ] <u>pizz</u>a
- [ ] wine

2 Work with a partner. Cover the words. Look at the pictures. Ask and answer questions.

What's this?

It's meat.

Colours

Match the colours with the words.

- [2] black
- [ ] blue
- [ ] brown
- [ ] green
- [ ] grey
- [ ] <u>or</u>ange
- [ ] pink
- [ ] red
- [ ] white
- [ ] <u>yell</u>ow

Common adjectives

Match the pictures with the words.

- [6] <u>beau</u>tiful
- [ ] big
- [ ] cheap
- [ ] ex<u>pen</u>sive
- [ ] small
- [ ] <u>ug</u>ly

5 Life

Grammar Present simple: *I, you, we, they*
Vocabulary Common verbs. Jobs
Useful phrases On the phone

Reading

1 Read and complete the questionnaire.

Your life
expectancy

Tick a or b.

1 You are:
a) male ♂ ☐   b) female ♀ ☐

2 You live in a big city (3 million people +):
a) Yes ☐   b) No ☐

3 You have old people in your family (75+):
a) Yes ☐   b) No ☐

4 You like your job:
a) Yes ☐   b) No ☐

5 You work:
a) inside ☐   b) outside ☐

6 You eat healthy food:
a) Yes ☐   b) No ☐

7 You sleep 6–8 hours:
a) Yes ☐   b) No ☐

8 You smoke:
a) Yes ☐   b) No ☐

How to score

1:	a) 2 b) 4	**5:**	a) 1 b) 2
2:	a) 2 b) 4	**6:**	a) 6 b) 2
3:	a) 6 b) 2	**7:**	a) 4 b) 2
4:	a) 8 b) 2	**8:**	a) 0 b) 8

Your score results

30 to 42: Your life expectancy is 100.
20 to 29: Your life expectancy is 75.
10 to 19: Change your life!

2 Compare your score and your answers with a partner.

Vocabulary

1 Complete the sentences with *eat, have, like, live, speak* or *work*.

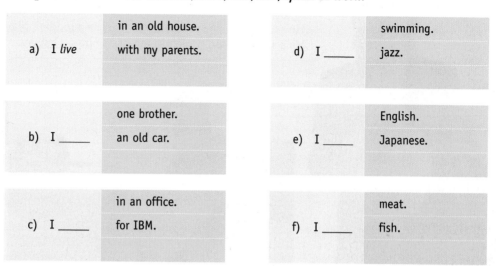

a) I *live*	in an old house.	
	with my parents.	

d) I _____	swimming.	
	jazz.	

b) I _____	one brother.	
	an old car.	

e) I _____	English.	
	Japanese.	

c) I _____	in an office.	
	for IBM.	

f) I _____	meat.	
	fish.	

🌐 **1.62** Listen, check and repeat.

2 Make more sentences. Use the phrases in the box.

healthy food   in a new apartment   my job   outside   Spanish   two children

3 Write six sentences about you. Use the verbs in Exercise 1.

I live in a big apartment.   I have three children.   I work ...

Grammar

Present simple:
I, you, we, they

I
You   **speak** English.
We   **don't speak** French.
They

Do you **speak** Chinese?
Yes, I **do**.
No, I **don't**.

1 Complete the answers.

a) 'Do you speak Chinese?'   'Yes, I *do*.'   'No, I *don't*.'
b) 'Do you smoke?'   'Yes, I *do*.'   'No, I _____.'
c) 'Do you and your family live in a city?' 'Yes, we do.'   'No, we _____.'
d) 'Do your friends like football?'   'Yes, they _____.' 'No, they don't.'
e) 'Do you eat meat?'   'Yes, _____.'   'No, _____.'
f) 'Do your parents have a dog?'   'Yes, _____.'   'No, _____.'

🌐 **1.63** Listen, check and repeat.

2 Work with a partner. Ask and answer the questions in Exercise 1.

3 Put the words in the correct order.

a) live / you / Where / do ? *Where do you live?*
b) Where / you / do / work ?
c) languages / you / speak / What / do ?
d) like / What / food / you / do ?
e) you / music / What / like / do ?
f) sports / do / What / like / you ?

🌐 **1.64** Listen, check and repeat.

4 Work with a partner. Ask and answer the questions in Exercise 3.

5 Grammar *Extra* 5 page 128. Read the explanation and do the exercises.

Vocabulary

1 **Match the sentences about jobs with the photos (*a–f*).**

> He's a <u>pi</u>lot.   She's a mu<u>si</u>cian.   He's a <u>foot</u>ball <u>play</u>er.
> He's a <u>ta</u>xi <u>driver</u>.   He's an <u>ar</u>tist.   She's a <u>law</u>yer.

a

b

c

d

e

f

🌐 **1.65** **Listen, check and repeat.**

2 🌐 **1.66** **Listen and repeat more sentences about jobs.**

a) 'I'm a <u>flight</u> at<u>ten</u>dant.'   b) 'I'm a <u>doc</u>tor.'   c) 'I'm a <u>se</u>cretary.'

d) 'I'm a <u>farm</u>er.'   e) 'I'm a <u>shop</u> as<u>sis</u>tant.'   f) 'I'm a <u>jour</u>nalist.'

3 **Who says it? Match the sentences with the jobs in Exercise 2.**

a) 'I work **in** a hospital.' *A doctor.*   d) 'I work **for** British Airways.'
b) 'I work **in** an office.'   e) 'I work **for** *Hello* magazine.'
c) 'I work **in** a shop.'   f) 'I work outside.'

🌐 **1.67** **Listen, check and repeat.**

4   **Pairwork** **Student A:** page 117 **Student B:** page 122

Pronunciation

1 🔘 1.68 **Listen and repeat the *Wh* questions. Notice the <u>stress</u>.**

A	B	C
<u>Where</u> are you <u>from</u>?	What <u>drinks</u> do you <u>like</u>?	<u>What's</u> your favourite <u>colour</u>?
<u>Where</u> do you <u>live</u>?	What <u>car</u> do you <u>have</u>?	<u>Who's</u> your favourite <u>actor</u>?
<u>Where</u> do you <u>work</u>?	What <u>music</u> do you <u>like</u>?	<u>What's</u> your favourite <u>city</u>?
<u>What</u> do you <u>do</u>?	What <u>sports</u> do you <u>like</u>?	<u>What's</u> your favourite <u>food</u>?

2 **Write two more *Wh* questions.**

Practise the questions.

Listening

1 🔘 1.69 **Listen to interviews with five people (*1–5*). Put the number of each person next to their real job and their dream job.**

Real job

taxi driver	☐
actor	☐
lawyer	☐
teacher	1
student	☐

Dream job

doctor	☐
DJ	☐
pilot	☐
football player	☐
actor	☐
musician	1

2 **Complete the two questions from the interviews.**
a) What _____ you _____?
b) What's _____ dream _____?

🔘 1.70 **Listen, check and repeat.**

Speaking

Ask questions and find out the real jobs and the dream jobs of three people in the class.

Alberto, what do you do?

I'm a teacher.

What's your dream job?

Model.

Useful phrases

1 ⊕ 1.71 **Read, listen and match the conversations (*a* and *b*) to the pictures (*1* and *2*).**

a) A: Good morning. British Airways.
   B: Oh, good morning. Can I speak to Mr Jones, please?
   A: Hold on a minute, please. ... I'm sorry. Mr Jones is out.
   B: Oh, OK. Thank you. Goodbye.

b) C: Hello.
   D: Hello. Can I speak to Janet, please?
   C: Hold on a minute. JANET!! I'm sorry. She's out.
   D: Oh, OK. Thanks. Bye.

2 ⊕ 1.72 **Listen and repeat the useful phrases.**

a) Can I speak to Mr Jones, please?
b) Hold on a minute, please.
c) I'm sorry. He's out.

3 **Work with a partner. Write a similar phone conversation for one of these situations.**

a) You phone your friend Tom at his house. He's out.
b) You phone a bank and want to speak to the manager, Mrs Brown. She's out.

Practise the conversation.

Vocabulary *Extra*

Jobs

1 Match the pictures with the words.

- ☐3 an <u>ac</u>tor
- ☐ an <u>ar</u>tist
- ☐ a DJ
- ☐ a <u>doc</u>tor
- ☐ a <u>far</u>mer
- ☐ a <u>flight</u> at<u>ten</u>dant
- ☐ a <u>foot</u>ball <u>play</u>er
- ☐ a <u>jour</u>nalist
- ☐ a <u>law</u>yer
- ☐ a mu<u>si</u>cian
- ☐ a <u>pi</u>lot
- ☐ a <u>sec</u>retary
- ☐ a <u>shop</u> as<u>sist</u>ant
- ☐ a <u>taxi</u> <u>dri</u>ver
- ☐ a <u>tea</u>cher

2 Work with a partner. Cover the words. Look at the pictures. Ask and answer questions.

What does he do?

He's a farmer.

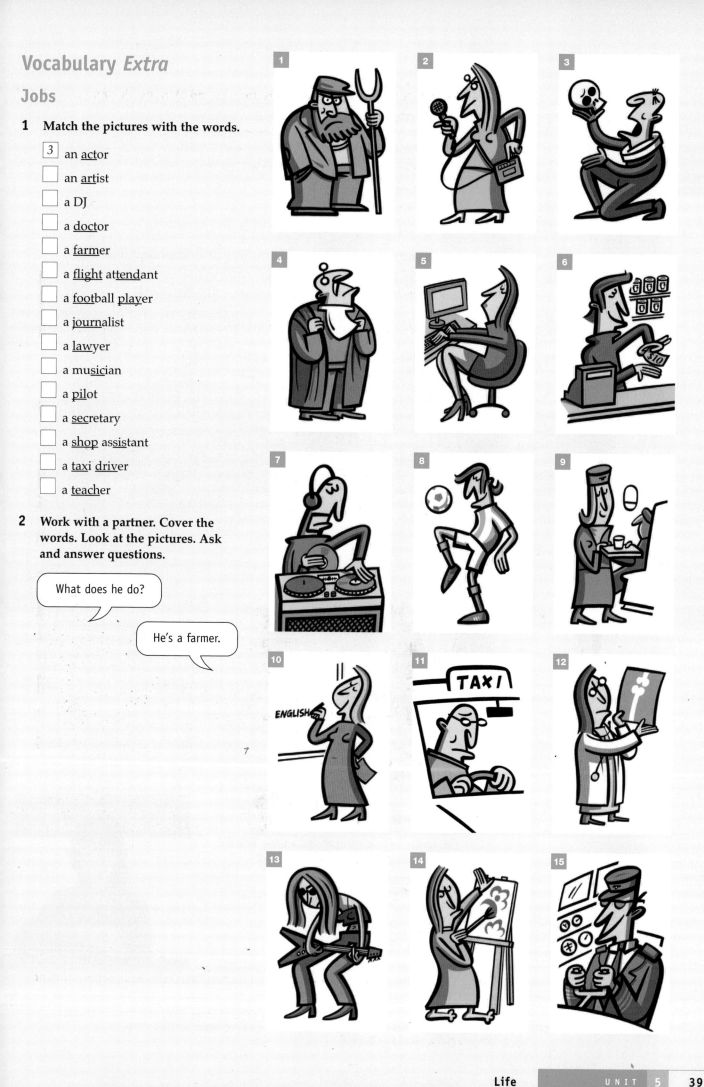

6 24/7

Grammar The time. Present simple: *he*, *she*, *it*
Vocabulary Days. Daily routine. Verb phrases with *get*, *go*, *have*
Useful phrases Greetings

Listening

1 🌐 **1.73 Listen and complete the times on the map of international time zones.**

a) San Francisco *4.00 a.m.*   c) London   e) Hong Kong
b) Buenos Aires   d) Moscow   f) Wellington

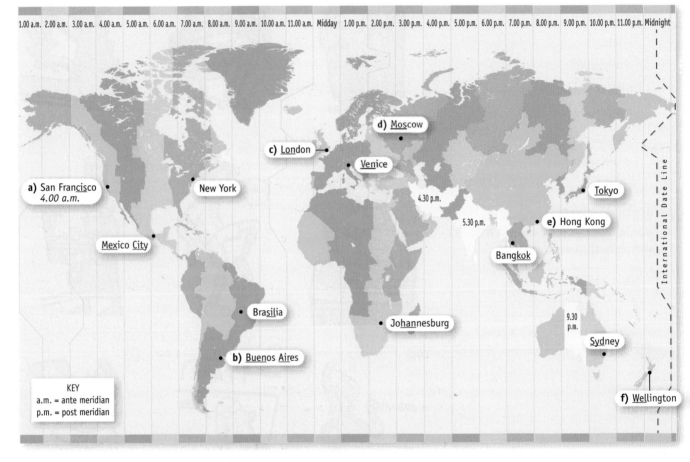

1.00 a.m. 2.00 a.m. 3.00 a.m. 4.00 a.m. 5.00 a.m. 6.00 a.m. 7.00 a.m. 8.00 a.m. 9.00 a.m. 10.00 a.m. 11.00 a.m. Midday 1.00 p.m. 2.00 p.m. 3.00 p.m. 4.00 p.m. 5.00 p.m. 6.00 p.m. 7.00 p.m. 8.00 p.m. 9.00 p.m. 10.00 p.m. 11.00 p.m. Midnight

d) Moscow
c) London
Venice
a) San Francisco 4.00 a.m.
New York
4.30 p.m.
Tokyo
5.30 p.m.
e) Hong Kong
Mexico City
Bangkok
Brasilia
Johannesburg
9.30 p.m.
Sydney
b) Buenos Aires
f) Wellington
International Date Line

KEY
a.m. = ante meridian
p.m. = post meridian

2 Complete the table.

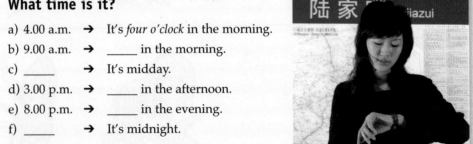

What time is it?

a) 4.00 a.m. → It's *four o'clock* in the morning.
b) 9.00 a.m. → _____ in the morning.
c) _____ → It's midday.
d) 3.00 p.m. → _____ in the afternoon.
e) 8.00 p.m. → _____ in the evening.
f) _____ → It's midnight.

🌐 **1.74 Listen, check and repeat.**

3 🌐 **1.75 Listen and repeat the names of the other cities on the map.**

Grammar

The time

What time is it?

It's three o'clock.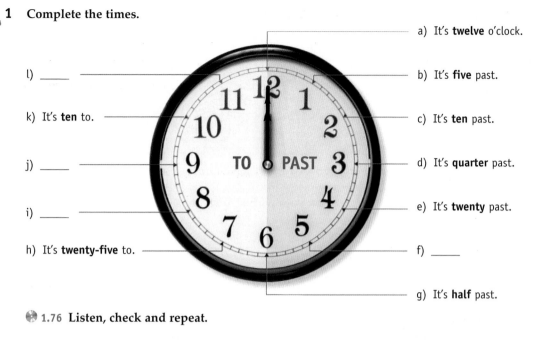

It's half past six.

It's quarter to twelve.

1 **Complete the times.**

a) It's **twelve** o'clock.

b) It's **five** past.

c) It's **ten** past.

d) It's **quarter** past.

e) It's **twenty** past.

f) _____

g) It's **half** past.

l) _____

k) It's **ten** to.

j) _____

i) _____

h) It's **twenty-five** to.

TO   PAST

1.76 **Listen, check and repeat.**

2 **Complete the times.**

a) It's two thirty.   `2:30`   *It's half past two.*

b) *It's seven fifty.*   `7:50`   It's ten to eight.

c) _____   `3:35`   It's twenty-five to four.

d) It's ten fifteen.   `10:15`   _____

e) It's five-oh-five.   `5:05`   _____

f) _____   `12:45`   It's quarter to one.

1.77 **Listen, check and repeat.**

3 **Say a time. Your partner says the same time in a different way.**

Nine twenty.   It's twenty past nine.

4 **Look at the time zones on page 40 and answer the questions.**

a) It's half past nine in the morning in Tokyo. What time is it in Venice?

b) It's twenty to six in the evening in Brasilia. What time is it in Moscow?

c) It's ten past two in the afternoon in Bangkok. What time is it in Johannesburg?

Ask your partner similar questions.

Vocabulary

Days of the week

Monday   Friday
Tuesday   Saturday
Wednesday   Sunday
Thursday

1 1.78 **Listen and repeat the days of the week.**

2 **Say a day of the week. Your partner says the next three days.**

Tuesday.   Wednesday, Thursday, Friday.

Vocabulary

1 🌐 1.79 Listen and repeat the verb phrases.

get up   have a shower   go to work   have lunch   finish work   get home   have dinner   go to bed

2 Ask your partner questions with *What time do you ...?*

> What time do you get up on Mondays?

> At seven o'clock.

Reading

1 🌐 1.80 Read an article about DJ Judge Jules. Answer the questions.

a) Where does he work?
b) What's the name of his favourite club?

MY DAY
MY NIGHT

ON WEEKDAYS
I (1) *get* up early, have breakfast and take my son to school. Then I go to the gym. After that I (2) _____ to work in a recording studio. I finish work at 6.00 p.m. and (3) _____ dinner with my family. We have two young children, Jake and Phoebe. So we (4) _____ to bed early.

ON SATURDAYS
I (5) _____ to bed in the afternoon and then I (6) _____ to work in the evening. I work all night in a club. My favourite club is Gatecrasher in Liverpool, but I work in clubs all round the world. Visit my website at www.judgejules.net for club dates. I work hard, but I also (7) _____ a good time.

ON SUNDAYS
I (8) _____ home in the morning, (9) _____ a shower and (10) _____ lunch with my family. In the afternoon I relax. I listen to music and play with my children.

2 Complete the text with *get, go* or *have*.

Read and check.

3 Look at these sentences about Judge Jules. Are they true or false?

a) On weekdays he gets up early.
b) On weekdays he takes his son to school.
c) On weekdays he goes to bed in the afternoon.
d) On Saturdays he finishes work at 6.00 p.m.
e) On Saturdays he works all night.
f) On Sundays he has lunch with his family.

Grammar

Present simple: *he, she, it*

He **works** all night.
He **doesn't work** at home.
(doesn't = does **not**)

Does she **like** club music?
Yes, she **does**.
No, she **doesn't**.

1 **Complete the questions and answers about Judge Jules.**

a) 'Does he go to the gym on weekdays?'   'Yes, he *does*.'   'No, he *doesn't*.'
b) 'Does he have children?'   'Yes, he _____ .'   'No, he _____ .'
c) 'Does he go to bed in the evening on Saturdays?'   'Yes, he _____ .'   'No, he _____ .'
d) '_____ he work in clubs all round the world?'   '_____ .'   '_____ .'
e) '_____ he like his job?'   '_____ .'   '_____ .'
f) '_____ he get home in the evening on Sundays?'   '_____ .'   '_____ .'

🌐 **1.81 Listen, check and repeat.**

2 **Work with a partner. Ask and answer the questions in Exercise 1.**

3   Grammar *Extra* 6 page 128. Read the explanation and do the exercises.

4   Pairwork   **Student A:** page 117   **Student B:** page 122

Pronunciation

1   🌐 1.82 **Listen and repeat the verbs.**

A Same number of syllables with *he/she/it*	B Extra syllable with *he/she/it*
do – does get – gets go – goes have – has	finish – finishes relax – relaxes

2   🌐 1.83 **Listen, repeat and add these verbs to the table in Exercise 1.**

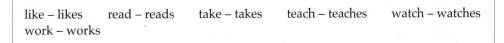

like – likes   read – reads   take – takes   teach – teaches   watch – watches
work – works

24/7

Useful phrases

1 🔊 1.84 **Read and listen to the phone conversation. Answer the questions.**

a) What time is it in New York?

b) What time is it in Sydney?

Mr Edwards: Hello.
John: Good morning! Is that Mr Edwards?
Mr Edwards: Who is this?
John: It's John from New York.
Mr Edwards: What time is it in New York, John?
John: It's 8.30 in the morning.
Mr Edwards: Oh. Do you know what time it is in Sydney, John?
John: Er, no. What time is it in Sydney, Mr Edwards?
Mr Edwards: It's 11.30 ... p.m.
John: Oh, good evening, Mr Edwards.
Mr Edwards: Goodnight, John.

Practise the conversation.

2 **Complete with** *Hello* **or** *Goodbye.*

Good morning.
Good afternoon. } = a) _____   Goodnight. = b) _____
Good evening.

🔊 1.85 **Listen and repeat the useful phrases.**

3 **Work with a partner. Complete a similar phone conversation between Mrs Harper in Los Angeles and her secretary, Jenny, in London.**

Mrs Harper: Hello.
Jenny: Good afternoon! Is that Mrs Harper?
Mrs Harper: Who is this?
Jenny: It's Jenny ...

Practise the conversation.

Vocabulary *Extra*

The day

Match the pictures with the words.

- [3] mor<u>ni</u>ng
- [ ] mid<u>day</u>
- [ ] after<u>noo</u>n
- [ ] <u>e</u>vening
- [ ] <u>mid</u>night
- [ ] night

Daily routine

1 Match the pictures with words

- [9] <u>fin</u>ish work
- [ ] get home
- [ ] get up
- [ ] go to bed
- [ ] go to work
- [ ] have a <u>shower</u>
- [ ] re<u>lax</u>
- [ ] <u>study</u>
- [ ] watch TV

2 When do you do these things?

Morning	*get up*
Afternoon	
Evening	
Night	

Review B

Grammar

▶ Grammar *Extra* pages 128 and 129

1 Make sentences with *I like* or *I don't like*. Use two words in the box for each picture.

> ~~big~~ black cheap ~~cities~~ coffee dogs
> expensive films old pens small wine

a) I don't like big cities.

Tick (✓) the sentences that are true for you.

2 Write a question for each sentence.

a) Do you like big cities?

Ask and answer the questions with a partner.

3 Complete the questions with *What*, *Where* or *Who*.

a) _____ do you live?
b) _____ languages do you speak?
c) _____ do you work?
d) _____ food do you like?
e) _____ 's your favourite singer?
f) _____ sports do you like?

Work with a partner. Ask and answer the questions.

4 Match the times with the same meaning.

a) It's six thirty-five. ⎤ 1 It's quarter to six.
b) It's four ten.   ⎟ 2 It's twenty past eleven.
c) It's eleven twenty.   ⎬ 3 It's ten to five.
d) It's five forty-five. ⎟ 4 It's quarter past twelve.
e) It's four fifty.   ⎟ 5 It's ten past four.
f) It's twelve fifteen. ⎦ 6 It's twenty-five to seven.

Compare your answers with a partner.

5 Complete the description of Aiko's day. Use the verbs in the box in the correct form.

> finish get get go go have have
> have ~~work~~ work

Aiko (1) *works* for an airline. She (2) _____ up at half past ten in the morning. She (3) _____ a shower at quarter to eleven. She (4) _____ to work at quarter past eleven.
She (5) _____ lunch at quarter to two. She (6) _____ for six more hours. She (7) _____ dinner at nine o'clock in the evening. She (8) _____ work at quarter past ten. She (9) _____ home at half past eleven at night. She (10) _____ to bed at one o'clock in the morning.

6 Spot the mistake! Cross out the incorrect sentence, *a* or *b*.

1 a) ~~'Do you like pizza?' 'Yes, I like.'~~
   b) 'Do you like pizza?' 'Yes, I do.'

2 a) I like Spanish films.
   b) I like films Spanish.

3 a) We no speak Chinese.
   b) We don't speak Chinese.

4 a) It's fifteen past one.
   b) It's quarter past one.

5 a) Does she like music?
   b) Does she likes music?

6 a) My mum gets up at 6 a.m.
   b) My mum get up at 6 a.m.

Vocabulary

1 <u>Underline</u> the 'odd word out' in each group.

a) Chinese food   <u>swimming</u>   Italian food
b) tennis   football   meat
c) wine   fish   spaghetti
d) fruit   Coke   coffee
e) tea   pizza   pasta

2 Complete the descriptions with the colours in the box.

> blue   ~~brown~~   green   grey   orange   pink
> red   yellow

1 a *brown* bag   2 a _____ pen

3 an _____ mobile   4 a _____ diary

5 a _____ book   6 a _____ pencil

7 a _____ eraser   8 a _____ iPod

3 Complete the crossword with the colours in Exercise 2.

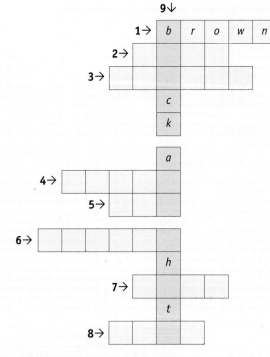

Which two colours are in 9?

4 Make the sentences true for you. Use the verbs in the box. Add *don't* where necessary.

> ~~eat~~   have   like   live   speak   work

a) I (*don't*) *eat* meat.   d) I _____ for a company.
b) I _____ jazz.   e) I _____ with my parents.
c) I _____ a sister.   f) I _____ Italian.

Compare your answers with a partner.

5 Complete the names of the jobs (*a–f*).

a) t a x i d r i v e r   d) __ rt __ st
b) d __ ct __ r   e) j __ __ rn __ l __ st
c) l __ wy __ r   f) fl __ ght __ tt __ nd __ nt

6 Complete the questions with the phrases in the box.

> get home   ~~get up~~   go to bed   go to work
> have a shower   have lunch

'On weekdays …

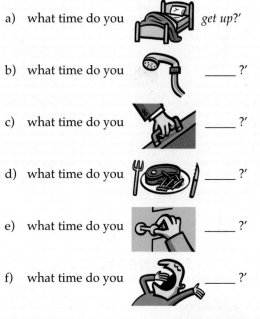

a) what time do you   *get up*?'

b) what time do you   _____ ?'

c) what time do you   _____ ?'

d) what time do you   _____ ?'

e) what time do you   _____ ?'

f) what time do you   _____ ?'

Work with a partner. Ask and answer the questions.

Pronunciation

1 Look at some words from Units 4–6. Say the words and add them to the table.

> ~~Brazil~~   ~~expensive~~   ~~France~~   gets   Madrid
> musician   o'clock   relaxes   smokes   ~~taxi~~
> watches   Wednesday

A: ☐	B: ☐☐	C: ☐☐	D: ☐☐☐
France	<u>*taxi*</u>	*Brazil*	*exp<u>en</u>sive*

2 <u>Underline</u> the stressed syllable in each word.

🔊 **1.86** **Listen, check and repeat.**

Reading & Listening

1 🌐 1.87 **Read the text. <u>Underline</u> the correct information.**

a) Dan lives in: (1) the USA (2) Britain (3) Spain.

b) Dan has: (1) a dog (2) a house (3) a daughter.

c) Dan works in: (1) a school (2) a hotel (3) a club.

d) In the afternoon Dan: (1) takes Anna to school (2) plays his guitar (3) sleeps.

e) Dan goes to the club after: (1) dinner (2) a shower (3) *The Simpsons.*

My life
Dan Hovey

Hi. My name's Dan. I'm a musician. I play the guitar in a big jazz club in New York. I live in a small apartment with my wife,
5 Lisa, and my daughter, Anna. Anna has a cat. Her name is Smudge. I like cats, but I don't like dogs.

My day

On weekdays, we wake up early and we have breakfast. Lisa goes to work at 7.00 a.m. She works at The Four Seasons hotel.
10 I take Anna to school at 8.30. After that, I go back to bed and sleep. At 11.30 a.m. I get up, have a shower and have lunch.
In the afternoon, I play my guitar and I listen to music. Anna and Lisa get home at 4.00 p.m. and we relax and watch TV. Anna loves *The Simpsons*. At 6.00 p.m. we have dinner. Then I go to the club.
15 I finish work at 12.00 a.m. and go home to bed. At weekends, I finish work at 1.00 or 2.00 a.m. and get home very late. I work hard but I love my job!

2 🌐 1.88 **Listen to the conversation. Are the sentences true or false?**

a) Paula Fox works for a music magazine.

b) Paula Fox is in London.

c) It's three o'clock in the afternoon in New York.

d) *The Night Life* is a jazz club.

e) Dan's wife is English.

f) Dan likes London.

Correct the false sentences.

3 **Listen again and complete the information about Dan.**

Star
profile

Name:	*Dan Hovey*
Lives:	*New York*
Works:	_____
Speaks:	_____
Favourite musician:	_____
Favourite colour:	_____
Favourite city:	_____
Favourite food:	_____

Writing & Speaking

1 Complete the rules for *and* and *but* with the examples in the box.

> ~~I play my guitar *and* I listen to music.~~
> I like cats *but* I don't like dogs.
> I don't like classical music *but* I love jazz.
> I don't like coffee *and* I don't like tea.

a) You use *and* to join similar ideas. For example:

+ / + *I play my guitar and I listen to music.*

– / – _____

b) You use *but* to join contrasting ideas. For example:

+ / – _____

– / + _____

2 <u>Underline</u> the correct word in each sentence.

a) I like jazz **and** / **but** I don't like rap.

b) She has a computer **and** / **but** she has a camera.

c) He speaks Italian **and** / **but** he speaks English.

d) I eat fish **and** / **but** I don't eat meat.

e) We get up **and** / **but** we have breakfast.

f) I don't like yellow **and** / **but** I love red.

3 Join the pairs of sentences using *and* or *but*.

a) I watch TV. I relax. *I watch TV and I relax.*

b) I like tea. I don't like coffee.

c) I have one sister. I have one brother.

d) I speak English. I speak Chinese.

e) I don't have a dog. I have a cat.

f) I play the piano. I play the guitar.

Make the sentences true for you.

4 Complete the sentences about yourself. Use the information about Dan Hovey's day on page 48 to help you.

My life

Hi. My name's _____ . I'm a _____ . I live _____ .

My day

On weekdays, I _____ in the morning and I _____ .
After that, I _____ and I _____ .
In the evening, I _____ and I _____ .
At weekends, I _____ , but I don't _____ .

5 Work with a partner. Ask questions with the question forms in the box.

> Where do you ...?   Who's your ...?
> What do you ...?   What's your ...?

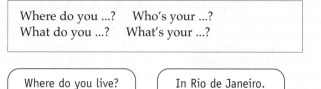

Where do you live?   In Rio de Janeiro.

Complete the form with your partner's information.

Star profile

Name: *Paula da Silva*
Lives: *Rio de Janeiro*
Works: _____
Speaks: _____
Favourite musician: _____
Favourite city: _____
Favourite colour: _____
Favourite food: _____

6 Write about your partner using the information in their *Star profile* in Exercise 5.

Paula da Silva lives in Rio de Janeiro. She ...

🎵 **1.89** **Song:** *Friday, I'm In Love*

7 NYC

Grammar *there is / there are. some/any*
Vocabulary Places in a city. Verb phrases with *go*. US and UK English
Useful phrases Asking about location

Vocabulary

1 Match the photos with the names in the box.

1 The Chrysler Building

> Brooklyn Bridge   Central Park
> ~~The Chrysler Building~~   Grand Central Station
> The Metropolitan Museum   Times Square
> The Statue of Liberty

🌐 2.01 **Listen, check and repeat.**

2 Work with a partner. What other famous places do you know in New York City?

3 🌐 2.02 **Listen and repeat the words.**

> a bridge   a <u>buil</u>ding   a lake   a mu<u>se</u>um
> a park   a <u>riv</u>er   a square   a <u>sta</u>tion
> a <u>sta</u>tue   a <u>the</u>atre

Find examples in the photos.

> There's a bridge in photo 6.

> There's a building in photo 1.

4 Write a list of famous places in your city or country.

> a bridge – Il Ponte Vecchio
> a building – Il Colosseo

5 Say the name of a famous place on your list. Your partner says what it is.

> Atocha.

> A station.

> El Prado.

> A museum.

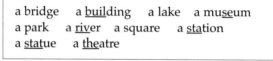

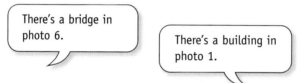

Reading

1 🌐 2.03 **Read and listen to three British people living in NYC. Match the descriptions (a–c) with the people (1–3).**

a) 'I love New York. I live **in** an old apartment **in** the East Village, **near** the university. I work **in** an office **near** the Hudson river. My favourite place **in** New York is Chinatown – I love Chinese food, and there are some fantastic restaurants.'

b) 'I love New York and I love Manhattan. I live (1) _____ a small apartment (2) _____ Washington Square Park. I'm a student but at the weekend I work (3) _____ a sports shop (4) _____ the Chrysler Building. My favourite place (5) _____ New York is the Hudson Hotel – the cocktails are very good.'

c) 'I love New York. I live (1) _____ an apartment (2) _____ the centre of Greenwich Village. I work (3) _____ a bank (4) _____ Grand Central Station. My favourite place (5) _____ New York is Central Park. I love sitting (6) _____ the lake, watching people.'

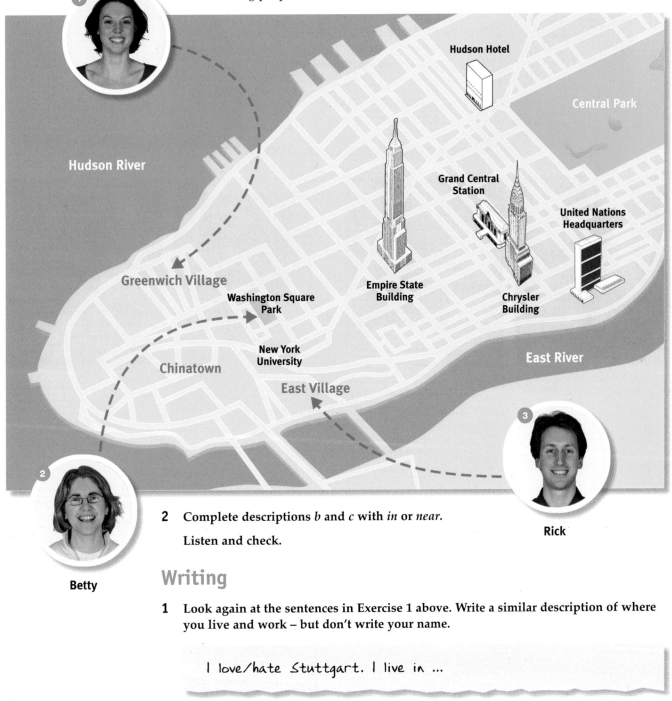

Emma

Hudson Hotel

Central Park

Hudson River

Grand Central
Station

United Nations
Headquarters

Empire State
Building

Chrysler
Building

East River

Greenwich Village

Washington Square
Park

New York
University

Chinatown

East Village

Betty

Rick

2 Complete descriptions *b* and *c* with *in* or *near*.

Listen and check.

Writing

1 Look again at the sentences in Exercise 1 above. Write a similar description of where you live and work – but don't write your name.

I love/hate Stuttgart. I live in ...

2 Read other students' sentences. Can you identify the student?

Reading & Writing

1 Read the webpage and choose your top thing to do in NYC.

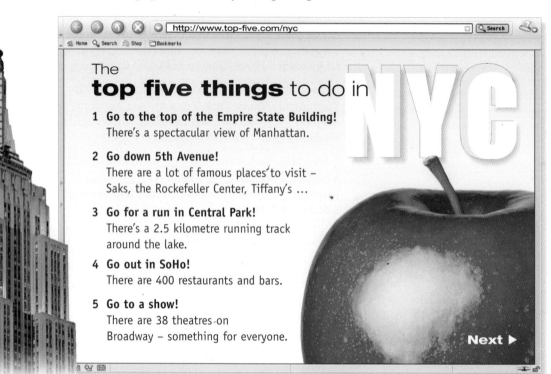

The
top five things to do in **NYC**

1 Go to the top of the Empire State Building!
There's a spectacular view of Manhattan.

2 Go down 5th Avenue!
There are a lot of famous places to visit –
Saks, the Rockefeller Center, Tiffany's …

3 Go for a run in Central Park!
There's a 2.5 kilometre running track
around the lake.

4 Go out in SoHo!
There are 400 restaurants and bars.

5 Go to a show!
There are 38 theatres on
Broadway – something for everyone.

Next ▶

2 Complete these sentences for a city in your country.

a) Go to the top of …   c) Go for a run in …   e) Go to …

b) Go down …   d) Go out in …

Compare with a partner.

Grammar

there is / there are

Singular
There's a museum.
There's an old statue.
(There**'s** = There **is**)

Plural
There are six cafés.
There are some nice bars.

1 Complete the information about Central Park with *There's* or *There are*.

a) *There's* a zoo.   d) _____ six cafés.

b) _____ 36 bridges.   e) _____ a museum.

c) _____ three restaurants.   f) _____ 25 million visitors every year.

🌐 2.04 **Listen, check and repeat.**

2 Write sentences about your city.

> There's a big church. There are some good restaurants.
> There's a big park …

Pronunciation

1 🌐 **2.05** **Listen and repeat the chants.**

A
There's a park.
There are some trees.
There are some statues.
There are some people.

B
There's a street.
There are some cars.
There are some buses.
There are some people.

2 Write and practise your own chant. Start with *There's a school ...* or
There's a restaurant ... or use your own ideas.

Grammar

Is there? / Are there?

Is there a park?
Yes, **there is.**
No, **there isn't.**

Are there any bars?
Yes, **there are.**
No, **there aren't.**

1 Complete the questions and answers.

a) 'Is there a station near your house?' 'Yes, *there is.*' 'No, *there isn't.*'
b) 'Are there any restaurants near your house?' 'Yes, there are.' 'No, there _____ .'
c) 'Is there a museum in your city?' 'Yes, there _____ .' 'No, there _____ .'
d) 'Is there a park near your house?' 'Yes, _____ .' 'No, _____ .'
e) '_____ there any hotels in your city?' '_____ .' '_____ .'
f) '_____ there a church near your house?' '_____ .' '_____ .'

🌐 **2.06** Listen, check and repeat.

2 Work with a partner. Ask and answer the questions in Exercise 1.

3 **Pairwork** **Student A:** page 118 **Student B:** page 123

4 Complete the table. Use the words in the box.

> airport   bars   beach   cinemas   hospital   river   schools   shops   square
> theatres

	✓ there's ...	✓✓✓ there are some ...	✗ there isn't ...	✗✗✗ there aren't any ...
Near my house	a beach			schools
In my city		shops	an airport	

Compare your answers with a partner.

5 **Grammar *Extra* 7** page 130. Read the explanation and do the exercises.

Useful phrases

1 Match the American English words with the British English words.

> British English: a cashpoint   ~~a chemist's~~   a toilet   an underground station

a) 🇺🇸 a pharmacy
   🇬🇧 *a chemist's*

b) 🇺🇸 an ATM
   🇬🇧 _____

c) 🇺🇸 a subway station
   🇬🇧 _____

d) 🇺🇸 a restroom
   🇬🇧 _____

🌐 **2.07 Listen, check and repeat.**

2 🌐 **2.08 Read and listen to two British tourists in New York. What do they ask for?**

Man:	Excuse me. Is (1) _____ a chemist's (2) _____ here?
Woman:	A chemist's?
Man:	Oh, sorry, a pharmacy.
Woman:	A (3) _____ ? Er, yes – over there.
Man:	Thanks.

Woman:	(4) _____ me. Is (5) _____ a toilet (6) _____ here?
Man:	A toilet?
Woman:	(7) _____ , a restroom.
Man:	A restroom?
Woman:	Yes, yes, a restroom.
Man:	A restroom? (8) _____ here? No.
Woman:	Oh!

3 Complete the two conversations in Exercise 2.

Listen and check.

4 🌐 **2.09 Listen and repeat the useful phrases.**

a) Excuse me. Is there a chemist's near here?
b) Yes – over there.

5 Work with a partner. Write a similar conversation about locating a cashpoint or an underground station.

Practise the conversation.

Vocabulary *Extra*

Town and country

1 Match the places in the picture with the words.

- 14 an a<u>i</u>rport
- ☐ a bar
- ☐ a beach
- ☐ a bridge
- ☐ a church
- ☐ a <u>ci</u>nema
- ☐ a lake
- ☐ a mu<u>se</u>um
- ☐ a park
- ☐ a <u>re</u>staurant
- ☐ a school
- ☐ a square
- ☐ a <u>sta</u>tion
- ☐ a <u>sta</u>tue
- ☐ a <u>the</u>atre

2 Work with a partner. Cover the words. Look at the places in the picture. Ask and answer questions.

What's this?

It's a lake.

8 Houses

Grammar Object pronouns
Vocabulary Rooms and furniture. Ordinal numbers
Useful phrases Offering a drink

Reading

1 **Look at two of Paul McCartney's houses.**

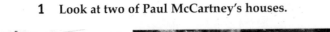

▲ 20 Forthlin Road, Liverpool   ▲ mansion in the USA

Match the plans below with one of the houses above.

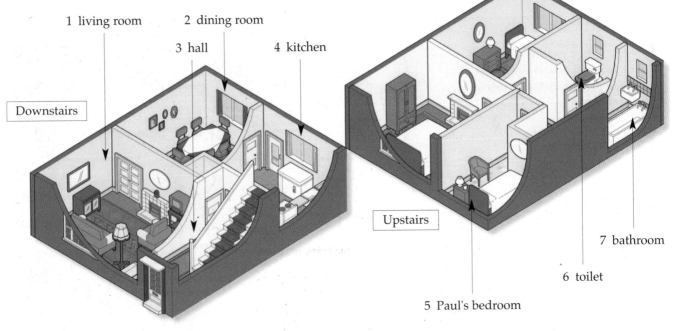

1 living room   2 dining room

3 hall   4 kitchen

Downstairs

Upstairs

5 Paul's bedroom

6 toilet

7 bathroom

🌐 2.10 **Listen and repeat the words in the picture.**

2 🌐 2.11 **Read and listen to a description of the house in Exercise 1.**

Paul McCartney – the early years

This small house was the home of the McCartney family. Downstairs, there's a (1) _____ , a living room, a dining room and a kitchen. (2) _____ , there are three bedrooms. (3) _____ is the small room above the front door. There's also a bathroom and a (4) _____ . The Beatles wrote their first number one hit *Love Me Do* in the (5) _____ . The house is a museum now, and thousands of tourists visit each year.

Complete the text with words from Exercise 1.

Listening & Vocabulary

1 🌐 2.12 **Listen to a description of Paul McCartney's house. Number the rooms in order (1–6).**

a) the living room ☐ c) the kitchen [1] e) the bathroom ☐

b) the dining room ☐ d) the toilet ☐ f) Paul's bedroom ☐

2 **Work with a partner. How many things can you name? Use the words in the box.**

> an <u>arm</u>chair a bath a bed a <u>car</u>pet chairs a <u>coo</u>ker a lamp a <u>show</u>er
> a sink a <u>so</u>fa a <u>ta</u>ble a <u>te</u>levision a <u>toi</u>let a <u>wash</u>ing ma<u>chine</u>

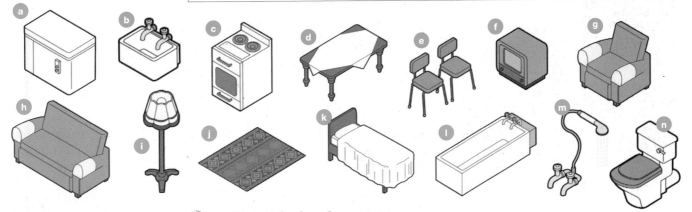

🌐 2.13 **Listen, check and repeat.**

3 **Look at the photos of Paul McCartney's house. Complete the sentences.**

▲ the kitchen

▲ the living room

a) There's a washing machine in *the kitchen*.

b) There's a carpet in _____ .

c) There's a bed in _____ .

d) There's a sofa in _____ .

e) There's a cooker in _____ .

f) There's a television in _____ .

🌐 2.14 **Listen, check and repeat.**

4 **Make more sentences about Paul McCartney's house.**

> There's an armchair in the living room.

▲ Paul's bedroom

5 Pairwork **Student A:** page 118 **Student B:** page 123

Reading

1 🌐 **2.15 Read the article. Match the people (*a–c*) with the places (*1–6*).**

Places we love and hate

Zainab Absullah (dancer)

'I love Paris. I don't like modern cities. The centre of Paris is very old and beautiful. I hate airports. They're big and ugly and hot.'

Antoine Boucher (chef)

'I love my kitchen. It's the best room in my house. I hate supermarkets. I do my shopping on the internet.'

Akane Ishimaru (writer)

'I love my bed. I sleep nine or ten hours every night. I hate the gym. I like walking or cycling.'

2   Match the questions with the answers.

a)	Does Zainab like Paris?	1	No, she hates it.
b)	Does Zainab like airports?	2	Yes, she loves it.
c)	Does Antoine like his kitchen?	3	No, he hates them.
d)	Does Antoine like supermarkets?	4	No, she hates them.
e)	Does Akane like her bed?	5	Yes, she loves it.
f)	Does Akane like the gym?	6	Yes, he loves it.

3   Which places do you love or hate? Tell your partner.

> I love my living room, but I hate my office.

> I love New York.

Grammar

Pronouns

Subject	Object
he	him
she	her
it	it
they	them

1 Complete the answers with *him*, *her*, *it* or *them*.

   a) 'What do you think of supermarkets?'   'I like *them*.'   'I don't like _____.'

   b) 'What do you think of your house?'   'I like _____.'   'I don't like _____.'

   c) 'What do you think of your city?'   'I like _____.'   'I don't like _____.'

   d) 'What do you think of your neighbours?'   'I like _____.'   'I don't like _____.'

   e) 'What do you think of David Beckham?'   'I like _____.'   'I don't like _____.'

   f) 'What do you think of Hillary Clinton?   'I like _____.'   'I don't like _____.'

   🌐 2.16 **Listen, check and repeat.**

2 Work with a partner. Ask and answer the questions in Exercise 1.

3 Make a list of places and famous people you love or hate.

   Ask your partner's opinion about the places/people on your list.

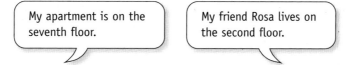

> What do you think of this school?

> I like it.

> What do you think of U2?

> They're OK.

4 ▌ Grammar *Extra* 8 page 130. Read the explanation and do the exercises.

Vocabulary

Ordinal numbers

 1st – first
 2nd – <u>second</u>
 3rd – third
 4th – fourth
 5th – fifth
 6th – sixth
 7th – <u>seve</u>nth
 8th – eighth
 9th – ninth
10th – tenth

1 🌐 2.17 **Listen and repeat the ordinal numbers.**

   Say the numbers round the class.

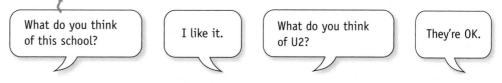

2 Look at the picture and complete the sentences.

   a) Mr and Mrs Robinson live on the *second* floor.

   b) Tina Brown lives on the _____ floor.

   c) Mr Taylor lives on the _____ floor.

   d) Robert Turner lives on the _____ floor.

   e) The Smiths live on the _____ floor.

   🌐 2.18 **Listen, check and repeat.**

3 Tell your partner about people in your apartment building or an apartment building you know.

> My apartment is on the seventh floor.

> My friend Rosa lives on the second floor.

Pronunciation

1 🌐 2.19 **Listen and repeat the sentences. Notice the pronunciation of 'th' (/θ/ and /ð/).**

	/ð/	/θ/
a) The Smiths live in Bath.	*The*	*Smiths, Bath*
b) Their apartment is on the fourth floor.		
c) Today is their third child's sixth birthday.		
d) Happy birthday, Samantha!		

2 Is 'th' pronounced /ð/ or /θ/? Complete the table.

Useful phrases

1 🌐 2.20 **Read and listen to the conversation. Answer the questions.**

a) What does Mrs Gregg offer Bryan?

b) What does Bryan want?

Mrs Gregg:	Hello, Bryan. Come in.
Bryan:	Hello, Mrs Gregg. Is Jo in?
Mrs Gregg:	Come in, come in.
Bryan:	Oh, OK, thanks.
Mrs Gregg:	Sit down.
Bryan:	Thanks. Er, is Jo ...?
Mrs Gregg:	Would you like a cup of tea?
Bryan:	No, thanks.
Mrs Gregg:	Would you like a cup of coffee?
Bryan:	Oh, no, thanks. Um, is Jo ...?
Mrs Gregg:	Would you like a glass of water?
Bryan:	No! ... I mean, no, thanks. Mrs Gregg. Where's Jo?
Mrs Gregg:	Oh, Jo's out. Now, would you like a ...

2 🌐 2.21 **Listen and repeat the useful phrases.**

a) Come in.

b) Is Jo in?

c) Sit down.

d) Would you like a cup of tea?

e) Jo's out.

3 **Work with a partner. Write a new conversation. Use different drinks.**

a beer   a cup of coffee   a glass of water

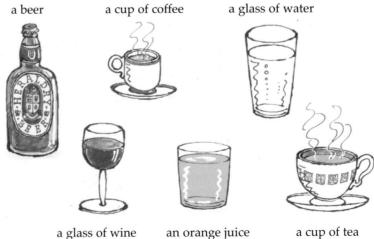

a glass of wine   an orange juice   a cup of tea

Practise the conversation.

Vocabulary *Extra*

Rooms

Match the rooms in the picture with the words.

2 the <u>bed</u>room

4 the <u>dining</u> room

3 the <u>kit</u>chen

5 the <u>living</u> room

1 the <u>bath</u>room

Furniture

1 Match the pictures with the words.

7 an <u>arm</u>chair

☐ a bath

☐ a bed

☐ a <u>carpet</u>

☐ a chair

☐ a <u>cooker</u>

☐ a lamp

☐ a <u>shower</u>

☐ a sink

☐ a <u>sofa</u>

☐ a <u>table</u>

☐ a <u>television</u>

☐ a <u>toilet</u>

☐ a <u>washing ma</u><u>chine</u>

2 Work with a partner. Cover the words. Look at the pictures. Ask and answer questions.

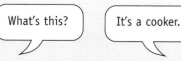

What's this? It's a cooker.

Diet

Grammar *How often ...?* Adverbs of frequency
Vocabulary Food. Drink. Time expressions
Useful phrases In a café

Reading

🔊 2.22 **Read the article. Which sentence (*a* or *b*) is true?**

a) With the 3-hour diet you eat three meals every day.
b) With the 3-hour diet you eat a meal every three hours.

Are your favourite things in this diet

The 3-hour diet

Women – do you want to eat ice cream and chocolate and have a body like Halle Berry? Men – do you want to eat bread and drink beer, and have a body like Brad Pitt? It's possible – with the new 3-hour diet!

It's not WHAT you eat but WHEN you eat. With the 3-hour diet, you have a small meal or a snack every three hours. It's possible to eat all your favourite things *and* lose one kilo a week!

Breakfast

Snack A

Lunch

Snack B

Dinner

Snack C

Breakfast	Snack A	Lunch	Snack B	Dinner	Snack C
1 cereal	6 milk	8 cola	13 tea	15 ice cream	20 cake
2 orange juice	7 chocolate	9 fruit	14 biscuits	16 beer	
3 coffee		10 chips		17 potatoes	
4 eggs		11 a hamburger		18 meat	
5 bread		12 salad		19 green beans	

Vocabulary

1 Complete the lists with words from the 3-hour diet. Write the words in each list in alphabetical order.

Drinks	Breakfast	Lunch/Dinner	Snacks
beer	*bread*	*chips*	*biscuits*

🔵 **2.23** Listen, check and repeat.

2 What food and drink do *you* have for breakfast, lunch, dinner, snacks? Tell your partner.

> I have coffee for breakfast. What about you?

> I have orange juice.

Grammar

How often ...?

How often do you drink coffee?

Every day.

1 Match *A* with *B*.

A
a) 7 a.m. 10 a.m. 1 p.m. 4 p.m. 7 p.m. 10 p.m.
b) Mon, Tues, Wed, Thurs, Fri, Sat, Sun
c) Mon a.m., Tues a.m., Wed a.m., Thurs a.m. ...
d) Saturday, Saturday, Saturday, Saturday ...
e) Week 1, Week 2, Week 3, Week 4 ...
f) Mon, Tues, Wed, Thurs, Fri, Sat, Sun

B
1 Every Saturday.
2 Every week.
3 Every three hours.
4 Every day.
5 Never.
6 Every morning.

🔵 **2.24** Listen, check and repeat.

2 Put the words in the correct order.

a) you / do / drink / How often / coffee ?
   How often do you drink coffee?
b) beer / How often / do / drink / you ?
c) you / do / tea / drink / How often ?
d) hamburgers / How often / do / you / eat ?
e) How often / eat / do / you / fruit ?
f) eat / chocolate / you / How often / do ?

🔵 **2.25** Listen, check and repeat.

3 Work with a partner. Ask and answer the questions in Exercise 2.

4 **Pairwork** **Student A:** page 118 **Student B:** page 123

Reading

1 🌐 2.26 **Read Mike's weblog. <u>Underline</u> the correct answer.**

a)   Mike <u>**loves**</u> / **hates** Thai street food.
b)   He <u>**says**</u> / **doesn't say** it's cheap and delicious.
c)   He **cooks** / <u>**never cooks**</u> at home.
d)   He <u>**has**</u> / **doesn't have** Thai soup for breakfast.
e)   His favourite dish <u>**is**</u> / **isn't** 'Pad Thai'.
f)   He **spends** / <u>**doesn't spend**</u> more than $4 a day.

Mike in Bangkok, Thailand

MY LIFE IN THAILAND

Street food in Bangkok

I love Thai street food – it's good and it's cheap and it's always delicious. I sometimes eat breakfast, lunch and dinner on the street in Bangkok. In fact, I never cook at home!

Breakfast
I start with fresh fruit: pineapple, watermelon or papaya. Then I have soup. Thai soup is very good. I usually drink water, but I sometimes have a cup of coffee.

Lunch
I usually start with orange juice. Then I have rice and eggs or rice and meat.

Dinner
I always have noodles for dinner. 'Pad Thai' is my favourite dish – it's really good. I usually drink Chang beer.

The street food in Bangkok is fantastic – I can have three healthy meals and I don't usually spend more than $4 a day.

2   **Which is your favourite international food? Tell your partner.**

| Chinese   French   Indian   Italian   Japanese   Spanish   Thai |

I love Japanese food. What about you?

My favourite is Italian food. I love pasta!

Grammar

Adverbs of frequency

100%	always
	usually
	sometimes
	not usually
0%	never

I **usually** drink water.

She does**n't usually**
eat meat.

1 **Look again at the text on page 64. Make sentences about Mike.**

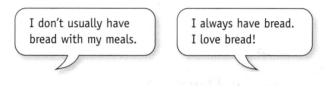

a) Mike never — 1 drinks beer with his dinner.
b) Mike sometimes 2 cooks at home.
c) Mike always 3 has noodles for dinner.
d) Mike usually 4 spend more than $4 a day.
e) Mike doesn't usually 5 has a cup of coffee for breakfast.

🌐 **2.27 Listen, check and repeat.**

2 **Complete the sentences about you with an adverb of frequency.**

a) I _____ have bread with my meals.

b) I _____ have sandwiches for lunch.

c) I _____ eat snacks between meals.

d) I _____ drink water with my meals.

e) I _____ cook lunch on Sundays.

f) I _____ eat food on the street.

Compare with a partner.

> I don't usually have
> bread with my meals.

> I always have bread.
> I love bread!

3 Grammar *Extra* 9 page 130. Read the explanation and do the exercises.

Pronunciation

1 🌐 **2.28 Listen and repeat the questions. Notice the vowel sounds (/ɪ/ and /iː/).**

a) Eat or drink? b) Fish or meat? c) Chips or beans? d) Tea or milk?

2 /ɪ/ or /iː/? **Complete the table to show the different vowel sounds.**

/ɪ/	/iː/
drink	

🌐 **2.29 Listen, check and repeat.**

Useful phrases

1 🌐 2.30 **Read, listen and complete the conversation.**

	small	medium	large		small	medium	large
Hot drinks				**Cold drinks**			
Coffee (regular)	$1.75	$2.25	$3.00	Iced tea	$2.00	$2.50	$3.25
Cappuccino	$2.75	$3.25	$4.00	Iced coffee	$1.75	$3.25	$4.00
Espresso	$2.00	$2.50	$3.25	Orange juice	$2.75	$2.25	$2.75
Americano	$2.75	$3.25	$4.00	Milk	$1.50	$2.00	$2.50
Tea	$2.00	$2.50	$3.25	Water	$1.75	$2.25	$2.75
Hot chocolate	$2.75	$3.25	$4.00				

Waiter: Next, please.

Andy: Can I have a cappuccino, please?

Waiter: Small, medium or large?

Andy: Just a minute, please.
(1) ~~Small~~ _____ or *large*?

Bess: Large.

Andy: (2) _No, Thanks_

Waiter: Sugar?

Andy: Just a minute, please. (3) _____ ?

Bess: No, thanks.

Andy: (4) _yes, please_

Waiter: Chocolate on top?

Andy: Just a minute, please.
(5) _____ _____ _____ ?

Bess: Yes, please.

Andy: (6) _____ , _____ .

Waiter: Anything else?

Andy: Yes. Can I have a medium Americano with sugar and no milk, please?

Waiter: OK. That's $7.25, please.

Andy: Here you are.

Waiter: Thank you. Next, please.

Listen again and check.

2 🌐 2.31 **Listen and repeat the useful phrases.**

a) Can I have a cappuccino, please?
b) Just a minute, please.
c) Anything else?
d) That's $7.25, please.
e) Here you are.

3 Work in groups of three. Write a similar conversation. Use the menu above.

Practise the conversation.

Vocabulary *Extra*

Food and drink

1 Match the pictures with the words.

- ⬜ 4 beer
- ⬜ biscuits
- ⬜ bread
- ⬜ cake
- ⬜ cereal
- ⬜ chips
- ⬜ chocolate
- ⬜ cola
- ⬜ egg
- ⬜ green beans
- ⬜ hamburger
- ⬜ ice cream
- ⬜ milk
- ⬜ noodles
- ⬜ orange juice
- ⬜ potatoes
- ⬜ salad
- ⬜ sandwich
- ⬜ soup
- ⬜ sugar
- ⬜ water

2 Write three things from Exercise 1 that you have for each of these meals.

- a) breakfast
- b) snack
- c) lunch
- d) dinner

Review C

Grammar

▶ Grammar *Extra* pages 130 and 131

1 Complete the sentences with *There's* or *There are*.

a) *There are* some good restaurants.

b) *There's* a park.

c) *There's* a theatre.

d) *There's* some hotels.

e) *There's* a museum.

f) *There's* some nice shops.

Rewrite the sentences as questions.

a) *Are there any good restaurants?*

b) *Is there a park?*

Write short answers to the questions about the area near your school.

a) *Yes, there are.*

Write a paragraph about the area near your school.

There are some good restaurants. There isn't a park. ...

2 Match the questions and answers.

a) Do you like cheese? — 1 No, I hate them.
b) Does she like chocolate? 2 Yes, I love it.
c) Does Manuel like dogs? 3 Yes, she loves it.
d) Do they like Thai food? 4 Yes, he loves it.
e) Do you like chips? 5 Yes, they love it.
f) Does he like beer? 6 No, he hates them.

3 Put the adverbs of frequency in order (1–5).

~~always~~ sometimes never not usually usually

100% ◄─────────────────► 0%

1 *always* 2 *usually* 3 *sometime* 4 *not usually* 5 *never*

Complete the sentences about you with an adverb of frequency.

a) I *usually* eat meat for lunch.
b) I *sometimes* drink coffee in the evening.
c) I *sometimes* have a banana for breakfast.
d) I *sometimes* have a snack in the morning.
e) I *usually* have noodles for dinner.
f) I *never* eat in bed.

Compare with a partner.

4 Write questions with *How often*.

a) you / eat apples *How often do you eat apples?*
b) you / drink milk
c) you / have a snack
d) you / eat Chinese food
e) you / drink Thai beer
f) you / buy fresh fruit

Ask and answer the questions with a partner.

Answer your partner's questions using the words in the box.

every day	every week	every morning
(four) times a day		(three) times a week
every (Saturday)	never	

5 Spot the mistake! Cross out the incorrect sentence, *a* or *b*.

1 a) ~~There some nice bars near my house.~~
   b) There are some nice bars near my house.

2 a) Is there bank near here?
   b) Is there a bank near here?

3 a) 'Does she like dogs?' 'Yes, she loves them.'
   b) 'Does she like dogs?' 'Yes, she loves it.'

4 a) How often do you eat fish?
   b) How often you eat fish?

5 a) I have always breakfast in bed.
   b) I always have breakfast in bed.

6 a) He no usually drinks beer.
   b) He doesn't usually drink beer.

Pronunciation

1 Look at some words from Units 7–9. Say the words and add them to the table.

~~biscuit~~	building	~~cereal~~	chocolate
~~delicious~~	fantastic	minute	museum
possible	potato	Saturday	theatre

A: ☐☐	B: ☐☐☐	C: ☐☐☐
biscuit	*cereal*	*delicious*

2 Underline the stressed syllable in each word.

🔊 2.32 Listen, check and repeat.

Vocabulary

1 Complete the crossword with the words for places (*1–9*) in a city.

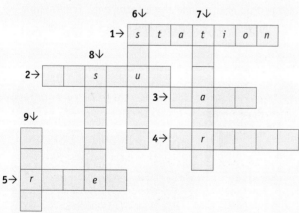

2 Complete.

1st	*first*	6th	_____
2nd	*s_____*	7th	_____
3rd	*t_____*	8th	_____
4th	_____	9th	_____
5th	_____	10th	_____

3 Match the British English and American English words.

> ~~cashpoint~~   chemist's   pharmacy   restroom
> subway   toilet   underground   ~~ATM~~

British	American
cashpoint	*ATM*

4 Complete the furniture words in each room.

a) bedroom: b*e*d l*a*mp c*a*rp*e*t

b) dining room: t_bl_ ch_ _rs

c) kitchen: c_ _k_r s_nk

d) living room: s_f_ _rmch_ _r

e) bathroom: b_th t_ _l_t

5 <u>Underline</u> the 'odd word out' in each group.

a) <u>potato</u> beer cola

b) egg breakfast banana

c) lunch noodles dinner

d) drink biscuit bread

e) soup cereal menu

f) tomato cake snack

Reading & Listening

1 🌐 2.33 **Read the descriptions of three homes in New York. Match Linda Sondstrum's dream home with one of the three homes (1–3).**

Nick Sutton **New York Properties**

Your dream home

Name	Linda Sondstrum	**Accommodation type**	Apartment
City	New York	**Bedroom**	2
Area	Centre	**Bathroom**	2
		Other	Big kitchen Near a park Near restaurants

Send ▶

1 Greenwich Village

A townhouse in the centre of New York. There are three bedrooms and two bathrooms. There's a small kitchen but a big dining room. The house is near Grand Central Station – near restaurants and cafés.

2 Central Park

A city centre apartment. There are two bedrooms and two bathrooms. There's a big kitchen and a big living room. The apartment is near Central Park and is ten minutes from Grand Central Station – near restaurants, cafés and theatres.

3 Queens

A large house in Flushing, Queens – thirty minutes from Grand Central Station. There are three bedrooms and three bathrooms. There's a big kitchen and a big dining room.

2 🌐 2.34 **Listen to Linda and the estate agent, Nick Sutton, and check your answer to Exercise 1.**

3 **Listen again. Are the sentences true or false? Correct the false sentences.**

a) Linda likes coffee.

b) The apartment is on the first floor.

c) It's in Manhattan.

d) There are two baths in the apartment.

e) There's a new cooker in the kitchen.

f) There are a lot of restaurants in the area.

Writing & Speaking

1 Complete *Your dream home* with your own ideas.

> http://www.newyork-properties.com   🔍 Search
>
> 🏠 Home 🔍 Search 🏠 Shop 📁 Bookmarks
>
> # Your dream home
>
> **Name** _____   **Accommodation type** _____
>
> **City** _____   **Bedroom** _____
>
> **Area** _____   **Bathroom** _____
>
> **Other** _____
>
> Send ▶

Compare with a partner.

2 Write a short description of your dream home.

My dream home is a sixth-floor apartment in the centre of Paris. It's near the Eiffel Tower. ...

10 Clothes

Grammar Present continuous
Vocabulary Clothes. Verb phrases
Useful phrases In a clothes shop

Listening & Vocabulary

1 Complete the descriptions with the colours in the box.

| black | blue | brown | green | grey | orange | red | white | yellow |

a
1 a *black* jacket
2 a *yellow* T-shirt
3 *blue* trousers
4 *black* shoes

b
1 a *blue* hat
2 a *green* top
3 a *brown* skirt
4 *red* boots

c
1 a *red* dress
2 *black* shoes

d
1 a *grey* suit
2 an *orange* tie
3 a *white* shirt
4 *black* and *white* trainers

⊙ 2.35 Listen, check and repeat.

2 ⊙ 2.36 Listen and match the names with the photos (*a–d*).

| Jasmine *c* | Kate *b* | Jason *d* | Leon *a* |

3 Ask questions and complete the table for your partner.

How often do you wear brown shoes?

Every day.

Every day	Sometimes	Never
brown shoes		

Reading

1 🔊 **2.37 Read the texts. Match the texts (a–c) with the photos (1–3).**

3 = a) Lola and Ana are receptionists in a hotel in Marbella so they always wear blue skirts and white tops. In this photograph it's fiesta time, so they're wearing traditional clothes. They're dancing and enjoying the sunshine.

1 b) Paolo and Elisa live in Verona, Italy. Paolo is a policeman, so he always wears a uniform for work. Elisa is a teacher and she usually wears trousers and a jacket. In this photograph, they're wearing costumes for the Venice carnival. They're having a great time.

2 c) Yuko is a university student. She's twenty years old and she lives with her parents in Okayama. She usually wears jeans, but in this photograph it's Adult's Day (Seijin-no-hi), so Yuko's wearing a kimono. She's holding a parasol.

2 **Complete the table with information from the texts.**

	Job	Clothes they usually wear	Clothes in the photo
Lola and Ana	*receptionists*	*blue skirts*	*fiesta costumes*
Paolo	*policeman*	*a uniform*	
Elisa	*teacher*	*trousers*	*a costume*
Yuko			

Grammar

Present continuous

I'm working
You're working
He's working
She's working
It's working
We're working
They're working

Are you working?
Yes, I am.
No, I'm not.

1 **Complete the questions and answers about the photos above.**

a) '*Are* Lola and Ana wearing blue skirts?'   'Yes, *they are.*' 'No, *they aren't.*'
b) '*Are* they dancing?'   'Yes, *They do* 'No, *They aren't*
c) '*Is* Paolo wearing a uniform?'   'Yes, *he is.*'   'No, *he isn't.*'
d) '*are* Paolo and Elisa having a great time?'   *yes she is* '*no she isn't*
e) '_____ Yuko wearing jeans?'   *yes she is* '*no she isn't*
f) '*is* she holding a parasol?'   *yes she is* '*no she isn't*

🔊 **2.38 Listen, check and repeat.**

2 **Work with a partner. Ask and answer the questions in Exercise 1.**

3 Pairwork **Student A: page 119 Student B: page 124**

4 Grammar *Extra* **10 page 132. Read the explanation and do the exercises.**

Pronunciation

1 🌐 **2.39 Listen and repeat the chants.**

A

<u>Teach</u>ing or <u>learn</u>ing?
<u>Stud</u>ying or <u>work</u>ing?
<u>What</u> are you <u>do</u>ing?
<u>What</u> are you <u>do</u>ing?

B

<u>Eat</u>ing or <u>drink</u>ing?
<u>Sleep</u>ing or <u>think</u>ing?
<u>What</u> are you <u>do</u>ing?
<u>What</u> are you <u>do</u>ing?

C

<u>Run</u>ning or <u>walk</u>ing?
<u>Listen</u>ing or <u>talk</u>ing?
<u>What</u> are you <u>do</u>ing?
<u>What</u> are you <u>do</u>ing?

2 **Write another chant. Use the verbs in the box.**

> buy / sell   come / go   give / take   read / write   sit / stand   stop / start

Practise your chant.

Listening

1 **Match the pictures (*a–c*) with the descriptions (*1–3*).**

1   A boy is playing on a PlayStation. His mother is phoning him from her office.
2   A woman is trying on clothes. Her husband is phoning her from his office.
3   A man is reading a newspaper. His wife is calling him from her office.

2 🌐 **2.40 Listen to three conversations. Match what the people are doing in the pictures (*a–c*) with what they *say* they are doing (*1–3*).**

1   'I'm making dinner.'
2   'I'm doing my homework.'
3   'I'm buying fish for dinner.'

Speaking

1 Work with a partner. Complete the conversations with your own ideas.

A: Where are you?
B: I'm on the train.
A: Where / go? *Where are you going?*
B: *I'm going to London.*

C: What are you doing, Dad?
D: I'm making dinner.
C: What / make? _____
D: _____

E: What are you doing?
F: I'm listening to music.
E: What / listen to? _____
F: _____

2 Practise your conversations.

Vocabulary

1 Complete the verb phrases with *do*, *play*, *read* or *make*.

| a) *do* | the housework |
| | the washing |

| b) _____ | a coffee |
| | a phone call |

| c) _____ | football |
| | the piano |

| d) _____ | a book |
| | an email |

🌐 2.41 Listen, check and repeat.

2 Make more verb phrases. Use the words in the box.

> dinner   on a PlayStation   a newspaper   your homework

3 Mime a verb phrase from Exercise 1. Your partner says what you are doing.

Useful phrases

1 🌐 2.42 **Read and listen to the conversation. Match it to picture** *a, b,* **or** *c.*

Shop assistant:	Can I help you?
Customer:	Yes, I'm looking for a dress.
Shop assistant:	A dress?
Customer:	Yes, a dress.
Shop assistant:	What size are you?
Customer:	It's for my wife.
Shop assistant:	What size is she?
Customer:	I think she's medium.
Shop assistant:	What colour?
Customer:	Red.
Shop assistant:	Do you like this one?
Customer:	How much is it?
Shop assistant:	It's £250.
Customer:	And how much is the blue dress over there?
Shop assistant:	It's £70.
Customer:	I prefer the blue dress.

2 🌐 2.43 **Listen and repeat the useful phrases.**

a) Can I help you?
b) Yes, I'm looking for a dress.
c) What size are you?
d) How much is it?
e) How much is the blue dress over there?

3 Work with a partner. Write a similar conversation for one of the other pictures.

Practise the conversation.

Vocabulary *Extra*

Clothes

1 Match the pictures with the words.

- [7] boots
- [ ] a dress
- [ ] a hat
- [ ] a jacket
- [ ] jeans
- [ ] a shirt
- [ ] shoes
- [ ] a skirt
- [ ] a suit
- [ ] a tie
- [ ] a top
- [ ] trainers
- [ ] trousers
- [ ] a T-shirt

2 Work with a partner. Cover the words. Look at the pictures. Ask and answer questions.

> What's this?

> It's a skirt.

> What are these?

> They're jeans.

11 Events

Grammar *be*: past simple
Vocabulary Months. Years. Dates. Adjectives
Useful phrases Buying tickets

Vocabulary

Months

01 – January
02 – February
03 – March
04 – April
05 – May
06 – June
07 – July
08 – August
09 – September
10 – October
11 – November
12 – December

1 🔊 2.44 **Listen and repeat the months.**
Ask your partner questions.

What's the third month?   March.

2 **Complete the table of famous birthdays.**

		You write	You say
a)	Bono	10th May	*the tenth of May*
b)	Paul McCartney	18th June	*the eighteenth of June*
c)	Neil Armstrong	5th August	_____
d)	Madonna	16th August	_____
e)	Ronaldo	22nd September	_____
f)	Prince Charles	14th November	_____

🔊 2.45 **Listen, check and repeat.**

3 **Write five birthdays in your family. You write:**
Me: 6th March
Say the birthdays to your partner. You say:

My birthday is the sixth of March.

4 **Match the years in numbers (*a–f*) with the years in words (1–6).**

a) 1969   1   two thousand and five
b) 1975   2   nineteen eighty-nine
c) 1989   3   nineteen sixty-nine
d) 1997   4   two thousand and six
e) 2005   5   nineteen seventy-five
f) 2006   6   nineteen ninety-seven

🔊 2.46 **Listen, check and repeat.**

5 **Write five years in numbers.**

1968   1973   ...   .

Dictate the years to your partner.

Check your partner's years.

Listening

1   🌐 2.47   **Listen and repeat the dates.**

> 22nd November 1963   20th July 1969   30th April 1975   9th November 1989
> 11th February 1990   6th September 1997   2nd July 2005   9th July 2006

2   **Match four dates in Exercise 1 with the events in the photos (*a–d*).**

SPECTACULAR
Television Events

a   Event: The 2006 World Cup final
TV audience: 3.5 billion (3,500,000,000)

b   Event: The Live 8 concerts
TV audience: 3 billion (3,000,000,000)

c   Event: Princess Diana's funeral
TV audience: 2.5 billion (2,500,000,000)

d   Event: The first Moon landing
TV audience: 500 million (500,000,000)

🌐 2.48   **Listen and check.**

3   **Work with a partner. Make a list of important events and dates for your country.**

Grammar

be: past simple

I **was**
you **were**
he **was**
she **was**
it **was**
we **were**
they **were**

Were you at Live 8?
Yes, I **was**.
No, I **wasn't**.
(wasn't = was **not**)

1 Complete the questions and answers.

a) *'Were* you at secondary school in 2002?'   'Yes, I *was*.'   'No, I *wasn't*.'
b) *'Were* you at work yesterday?'   'Yes, I ____ .'   'No, I ____ .'
c) '____ it sunny yesterday?'   'Yes, it ____ .'   'No, it ____ .'
d) '____ your mother born before 1963?'   'Yes, she ____ .'   'No, she ____ .'
e) '____ you and your friends in town yesterday?'   'Yes, we ____ .'   'No, we ____ .'
f) '____ your parents at university in 1975?'   'Yes, they ____ .'   'No, they ____ .'

🔊 **2.49** **Listen, check and repeat.**

2 Work with a partner. Ask and answer the questions in Exercise 1.

3 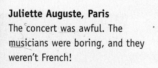 Pairwork   **Student A:** page 119   **Student B:** page 124

4 Grammar *Extra* **11** page 132. Read the explanation and do the exercises.

Reading

1 🔊 **2.50** **Read some opinions about the Live 8 concerts.**

a) Who was excited? yuko
b) Who was happy? olga
c) Who was lucky? amy
d) Who wasn't happy? Jul

Yuko Murayama, Tokyo
The concert was amazing. There were young people and old people. Japanese people are usually quiet, but we were very excited.

Gary Franz, Berlin
The bands were great. I love Green Day, and Brian Wilson was also fantastic – he is the Mozart of rock music.

Olga Ekareva, Moscow
The concert was in Red Square, near the Kremlin. It was great, and I was happy to be there.

Dawn Roberts, London
The concert was wonderful. Elton John was terrible, but Robbie Williams and Madonna were brilliant. I cried!

Juliette Auguste, Paris
The concert was awful. The musicians were boring, and they weren't French!

Randy Schwartz, Philadelphia
The concert was fantastic. The music was great, but the political message was more important.

Pietro Crucioli, Rome
The music was excellent. It was really hot. There was beer, but it was very expensive.

Amy Ronson, Ontario
Live 8 was amazing. I was lucky to have a ticket. There were a lot of people. It was like a carnival.

2 Read the opinions again. <u>Underline</u> the correct answers.

a) Japanese people <u>**were**</u> / **weren't** very excited.
b) In Paris the musicians **were** / **weren't** French!
c) It **was** / **wasn't** cold in Rome.
d) Brian Wilson **was** / **wasn't** fantastic.
e) Elton John **was** / **wasn't** terrible.
f) The political message **was** / **wasn't** important.

🔊 **2.51** **Listen, check and repeat.**

Vocabulary

1 Match the reactions to the Live 8 concert with the appropriate person. Put *A* for Andy or *C* for Cathy.

'It was amazing.' `A`   'It was awful.' `C`

'It was boring.' `C`   'It was excellent.' `A`

'It was fantastic.' `A`   'It was great.' `A`

'It was terrible.' `C`   'It was wonderful.' `A`

🌐 2.52 **Listen, check and repeat.**

Andy: 'It was amazing.'

2 Look at the opinions about Live 8 on page 80. Complete the sentences with an adjective from Exercise 1.

a) In Tokyo, the concert was *amazing*.

b) In Paris, the concert was _awful_.

c) In Rome, the music was _excellen_.

d) In Berlin, the bands were _fantastic_.

e) In London, the concert was _brilliant_.

f) In Philadelphia, the concert was _important_.

🌐 2.53 **Listen, check and repeat.**

Cathy: 'It was awful.'

3 Make sentences about you.

| I was at a | concert
party
wedding
restaurant
nightclub | last | night.
weekend.
week.
month.
year. | It was | ADJECTIVE. |

> I was at a concert last month. It was amazing.
> I was at my dad's birthday party last week. It was boring.

Compare your sentences with a partner.

Pronunciation

1 🌐 2.54 **Listen and repeat the adjectives in the box.**

amazing   delicious   excellent   expensive   fantastic   important
terrible   wonderful

2 Put the adjectives in Exercise 1 into list *A* or *B*.

A: ☐ ☐ ☐	B: ☐ ☐ ☐
excellent	*amazing*

Underline the stressed syllable in each word.

🌐 2.55 **Listen, check and repeat.**

Useful phrases

1 🌐 **2.56 Look at the Arts Centre Events web page. Then listen to the conversation and <u>underline</u> the correct answer.**

a) She wants to see <u>*Shrek*</u> / **Joao** / **Coldplay**.
b) She wants to buy **one ticket** / **two tickets** / **three tickets**.
c) She wants to pay **in cash** / **by cheque** / **by credit card**.

http://www.oxfordarts.com/boxoffice

🏠 Home 🔍 Search 🛍 Shop 🔖 Bookmarks

events | Arts Centre

Cinema	Adult £10 Child £5 Student £7 • **Monday 9th March to Saturday 14th March** *Shrek*: 3.30, 6.30 *War of the Worlds*: 2.30, 5.30, 8.30
Music	• **Thursday 12th March, Saturday 14th March** Club Havana: Joao – Bossa Nova and Latino £15 • **Friday 13th March, Saturday 14th March** Concert Hall: Coldplay £50
Tickets	Please phone the Box office on 01865 4371771.

2 Read, listen and complete the conversation with dates, times and numbers from the box.

> January 2012   6.30   ~~Friday 13ᵗʰ March~~.   Two   4899 2424 1836 5800   £20

Man:	Hello, Box office.
Woman:	Oh, hello. I'd like to buy tickets for *Shrek*, please.
Man:	When for?
Woman:	(1) *Friday 13ᵗʰ March*.
Man:	Friday 13ᵗʰ March. What time?
Woman:	(2) 6:30.
Man:	How many tickets?
Woman:	(3) two, please.
Man:	One adult, one child?
Woman:	Er, no, two adults.
Man:	That's (4) £20. How would you like to pay?
Woman:	By credit card, please.
Man:	Can I have your credit card number, please?
Woman:	(5) _____ .
Man:	Can I have the expiry date?
Woman:	(6) _____ .
Man:	Thank you.

Listen and check.

3 🌐 **2.57 Listen and repeat the useful phrases.**

a) I'd like to buy tickets for *Shrek*, please.
b) How many tickets?
c) How would you like to pay?
d) By credit card, please.

4 Work with a partner. Write a conversation for another event at the Arts Centre.

Practise the conversation.

Vocabulary *Extra*

Common adjectives

1 Match the pictures with the words.

3 <u>aw</u>ful

8 <u>bor</u>ing

2 de<u>li</u>cious

9 fan<u>tas</u>tic

5 good

7 great

10 <u>hap</u>py

4 im<u>por</u>tant

6 <u>luck</u>y

1 <u>ter</u>rible

2 Put the adjectives in Exercise 1 in the correct lists.

Positive (✓)	Negative (✗)
delicious	*awful*

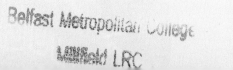

12 Hero

Grammar Past simple: affirmative forms
Vocabulary Sports
Useful phrases Special occasions

▲ Lance Armstrong

Vocabulary

1 🌐 2.58 **Listen and repeat the sports.**

> basketball   cycling   football   golf   sailing
> tennis

Match the sporting heroes (a–f) with their sports.

2 Add *go* or *play* to the sports in Exercise 1.
play basketball, go cycling, …

🌐 2.59 **Listen, check and repeat.**

▲ Pelé

Speaking

1 Make questions with *How often …?* Ask your partner.

> How often do you play basketball?

> Every Tuesday.

> How often do you go cycling?

> I never go cycling.

▲ Maria Sharapova

▲ Ellen MacArthur

2 What is your favourite sport? Who is your sporting hero? Tell your partner.

> My favourite sport is tennis.
> My sporting hero is Venus Williams.

▲ Tiger Woods

◀ Michael Jordan

Reading

1 🌐 **2.60** Read the article about Lance Armstrong. How many times did he win the Tour de France?

Lance Armstrong

The early years

Lance Armstrong was born on 18ᵗʰ September 1971 in Texas in the USA. His parents got divorced when he was a baby, and his mother remarried when he was three years old. He got his first bicycle in 1978.

5   He liked swimming and running, but his favourite sport was cycling. In 1988 he graduated from high school and joined the US Olympic team.

Professional life

In 1992, after the Barcelona Olympics, he became a professional cyclist. He lost his first important race in San Sebastian in Spain. He finished last!

10   But after that he won many important races and in 1996 he became the number one cyclist in the world.

After the 1996 Olympics in Atlanta, he had cancer. He had two operations and chemotherapy and finally, he recovered. Later, he started the Lance Armstrong Foundation and helped other people with cancer.

15   In 1998, he started racing again, and in 1999, he won the Tour de France for the first time. He won the Tour de France for the seventh time in 2005 and then retired.

Personal life

20   In 1997 he got married to Kristin Richard and had three children. After four years they got divorced, and in 2004 he started a new relationship with Sheryl Crow. They separated in 2006.

2 Put these events in Lance Armstrong's life in order (1–5).

a) He started a new relationship.   b) He got married.   c) He separated.   d) He got divorced.   e) He had children.

3 Complete the stages of Lance Armstrong's life with dates from the article.

a) He was born in *1971*.

b) He got his first bicycle in 1978.

c) He graduated from high school in 1988.

d) He became a professional cyclist in 1992.

e) He had cancer in 1996.

f) He got married in 1997.

g) He started racing again in 1998.

h) He won the Tour de France for the seventh time in 2005.

🌐 **2.61** Listen, check and repeat.

Grammar

Past simple

work + *ed*

I **worked**
you **worked**
he **worked**
she **worked**
it **worked**
we **worked**
they **worked**

1 Complete the table with the headings in the box.

Delete *y* and add *ied*   Add *ed* / *d*   Add consonant + *ed*

Past simple: spelling rules for regular verbs		
a) _____	b) _____	c) _____
talk → talked live → lived	study → studied	stop → stopped

Add these verbs to the table.

arrive   complete   cook   finish   join   like   phone   plan   recover
retire   talk   try   use   walk   watch

2 Complete the sentences about Lance Armstrong in the past simple.

a) He (like) *liked* swimming and running when he was a child.

b) He (join) _____ the US Olympic team in 1988.

c) He (finish) _____ last in his first important professional race.

d) He (recover) _____ from cancer after two operations and chemotherapy.

e) He (start) _____ a cancer foundation in 1997.

f) He (retire) _____ in 2005.

🌐 2.62 Listen, check and repeat.

3 Make sentences about yesterday.

a) I / use / a computer *I used a computer.*

b) I / walk / to work

c) I / plan / a holiday

d) I / listen / to music

e) I / cook / the dinner

f) I / study / English

🌐 2.63 Listen, check and repeat.

Tick (✓) the sentences that are true for you.

Pronunciation

1 🌐 2.64 Listen and repeat the present and past forms.

A		B	
Present	**Past**	**Present**	**Past**
help	helped	start	started
stop	stopped	wait	waited

Which verbs have an extra syllable in the past form?

2 Add the verbs to *A* or *B* in Exercise 1.

ask   hate   join   pass   play   point   want   watch

🌐 2.65 Listen, check and repeat.

Grammar

Past simple: irregular verbs

go – went

I **went**
you **went**
he **went**
she **went**
it **went**
we **went**
they **went**

1 🌐 2.66 **Listen and repeat the infinitive and past simple forms of these irregular verbs.**

a) go – went   send – sent   do – (did)
b) see – saw   wear – wore   know – knew
c) say – said   read – read   get – got
d) buy – bought   think – thought   write – wrote
e) speak – spoke   break – broke   take – took
f) tell – told   sell – sold   give – gave

Circle the past simple form which has a different sound in each group.

2 Pairwork **Student A:** page 119 **Student B:** page 124

3 Grammar *Extra* 12 page 132. Read the explanation and do the exercises.

4 **Complete the text about Juan Sebastián Elcano in the past simple.**

Juan Sebastián Elcano (1 be) *was* a Spanish explorer. He (2 be) _____ born in 1476 in the north of Spain. In 1522 he (3 complete) _____ the first voyage to sail round the world.

In 1519 the king of Spain (4 send) _____ an expedition to find a route to the East. Ferdinand Magellan (5 be) _____ the leader of the expedition, and he (6 ask) _____ Elcano to go with him. They (7 sail) _____ from Spain with five ships.

Magellan (8 die) _____ in the Philippines, but Elcano (9 continue) _____ the voyage. In 1522 only one ship (10 arrive) _____ back in Spain. 270 men (11 start) _____ the voyage in 1519, but only 18 men (12 return) _____ .

🌐 2.67 **Listen and check. Why is Juan Sebastián Elcano famous?**

Listening

1 🌐 2.68 **Listen and write down the order (*1–3*) in which these famous people are mentioned.**

Leonardo da Vinci   Beethoven   Mother Teresa

2 **Complete the sentences in the past simple.**

a) He (go) *went* deaf, but he (write) _____ wonderful music.

b) He (paint) _____ the Mona Lisa and he (design) _____ the first helicopter.

c) She (live) _____ a very simple life and she (give) _____ all her time and her love to poor people.

3 **Match the sentences with the famous people. Listen again and check.**

4 **Who is your hero in history? Tell a partner.**

Useful phrases

1 Match the special occasions (*1–6*) in the box with the greeting cards (*a–f*) below.

> 1 a birthday   2 a new baby   3 an important exam
> 4 a wedding anniversary   5 a new job   6 1ˢᵗ January

🔘 **2.69** **Listen and check.**

2 Complete the conversations with the messages in the box.

> Congratulations!   Happy birthday!   Good luck!

Ann: Look! I'm engaged.
Beth: _____ ! When's the wedding?
Ann: In April.

Cathy: Are you OK?
Dan: No. It's my driving test today.
Cathy: Oh, _____ !

Eric: It's my birthday today.
Fran: _____ ! How old are you?
Eric: Oh, 39 – again.

🔘 **2.70** **Listen and check.**

3 🔘 **2.71** **Listen and repeat the useful phrases.**

   a) Congratulations!   b) Good luck!   c) Happy birthday!

4 Work with a partner. Choose a situation from the box and write a conversation.

> You're 21 today.   You passed your exam.   You're in a race.

Practise the conversation.

5 What was the last special occasion you had? Tell your partner about it.

Vocabulary *Extra*

Verb phrases

1 Match the pictures with the words.

- [6] get di<u>v</u>orced
- [ ] get <u>ma</u>rried
- [ ] go <u>cy</u>cling
- [ ] go <u>sai</u>ling
- [ ] have an ope<u>ra</u>tion
- [ ] listen to <u>mu</u>sic
- [ ] lose a race
- [ ] play <u>bas</u>ketball
- [ ] play <u>foo</u>tball
- [ ] play golf
- [ ] play <u>ten</u>nis
- [ ] use a com<u>pu</u>ter
- [ ] watch TV
- [ ] win a race

2 Put the verbs in Exercise 1 into the past simple.

6 get divorced – got divorced

Review D

Grammar

▶ Grammar *Extra* pages 132 and 133

1 Look at the picture and complete the sentences with the verbs in the box. Use the present continuous.

Alice

Bella

Chris

Delia

Ed

Frank

| drink   eat   read   sleep   ~~speak~~   work |

a) Alice *is speaking* on the phone.

b) Bella _____ a cup of tea.

c) Chris _____ a newspaper.

d) Delia _____ at her computer.

e) Ed _____ a sandwich.

f) Frank _____ in his favourite chair.

2 Complete the questions with *Is* or *Are*.

a) *Are* Alice and Delia working?

b) _____ Bella speaking on the phone?

c) _____ Chris reading a newspaper?

d) _____ Frank and Ed drinking?

Answer the questions.

a) Yes, they are.

3 <u>Underline</u> the correct word.

Julia: (1) **Was / Were** you at home yesterday?

Dan: Yes, I (2) **was / were**. Why?

Julia: (3) **Was / Were** Joe with you?

Dan: No, he (4) **wasn't / weren't**.

Julia: (5) **Was / Were** Sara with you?

Dan: No, she (6) **wasn't / weren't**.

Julia: (7) **Was / Were** Kerry and Ben with you?

Dan: Yes, they (8) **was / were**. Why do you ask?

Julia: Oh, it's not important.

4 Complete the verb table.

Regular verbs		Irregular verbs	
Present	**Past**	**Present**	**Past**
stop	(1) _____	become	(5) _____
(2) _____	wanted	(6) _____	bought
finish	(3) _____	speak	(7) _____
(4) _____	studied	(8) _____	knew

5 Complete the sentences about the past.

a) I (be born) _____ in *Rome*.

b) When I was young I (have) _____ *a red bicycle*.

c) I (start) _____ at my first school in *1990*.

d) I (graduate) _____ from secondary school when I was *sixteen*.

e) On Monday I (go) _____ to *the cinema*.

f) Last night I (arrive) _____ home at *12.30*.

Change the words in *italics* to make the sentences true for you.

On Monday I went to <u>an Indian restaurant</u>.

Compare your sentences with a partner.

6 Spot the mistake! Cross out the incorrect sentence, *a* or *b*.

1 a) ~~I reading a really good book.~~
  b) I'm reading a really good book.

2 a) Is Paul working?
  b) Paul's working?

3 a) What you are doing?
  b) ~~What are you doing?~~

4 a) We wasn't happy with the hotel.
  b) We weren't happy with the hotel.

5 a) The car stopped near the school.
  b) The car stop near the school.

6 a) I taked the bus to work.
  b) I took the bus to work.

Vocabulary

1 Complete the crossword with the words for clothes.

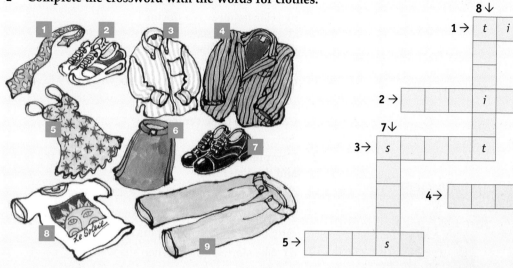

2 Complete the questions with *do, make, play* or *read*.

a) How many phonecalls do you _____ in a day?
b) How often do you _____ the housework?
c) Can you _____ the piano?
d) Do you _____ books in your free time?
e) How often do you _____ dinner?
f) Do you always _____ your homework?

Answer the questions.

Compare your answers with a partner.

3 <u>Underline</u> the correct word.

a) January is the **first** / **third** month.
b) February is the **second** / **sixth** month.
c) April is the **fourth** / **fifth** month.
d) October is the **seventh** / **tenth** month.
e) November is the **eighth** / **eleventh** month.
f) December is the **ninth** / **twelfth** month.

4 Complete the sentences with the months in the box. There is one extra month.

December February January July June
March

a) New Year's Day is 1st _____ .
b) Valentine's Day is 14th _____ .
c) Saint Patrick's Day is 17th _____ .
d) US Independence Day is 4th _____ .
e) Christmas Day is 25th _____ .

Read out your answers to a partner.

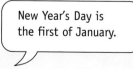

New Year's Day is
the first of January.

5 Look at the pictures and write sentences with the expressions in the box.

goes sailing   is playing football
went cycling   ~~played basketball~~   plays tennis

a) Andy / last week   *Andy played basketball last week.*
b) Britt / now
c) Carole / for her country
d) Dan / yesterday
e) Erica / every week

Pronunciation

1 Look at some words from Units 10–12. Say the words and add them to the table.

~~amazing~~   ~~audience~~   basketball   ~~cheque~~
fantastic   ~~football~~   helped   jacket   jeans
September   started   yesterday

A: □	B: □ □	C: □ □ □	D: □ □ □
cheque	*football*	*audience*	*amazing*

2 <u>Underline</u> the stressed syllable in each word.

🔊 2.72 Listen, check and repeat.

Reading & Listening

1 🌐 **2.73 Read the text about Lily Byrne. Put the events in order (1–6).**

a) She went to university. ☐

b) She had children. ☐

c) She became a doctor. ☐

d) She got married. ☐

e) She was born. 1

f) She went to school. ☐

My grandmother, Lily, is amazing!
  She was born on 6th May 1922, in
Ireland. She started school when she was
seven. Her parents were poor, but Lily liked
5 school and was a good student.
  She got married to my grandfather, Cyril
Murphy, when she was twenty years old.
They had a son and three daughters.
  She went to university in Dublin when
10 she was forty. She graduated from
university when she was forty-five and
became a doctor. She went to India and
worked in a hospital. She wanted to help
poor people.
15 Now Lily lives in Dublin again. She has
ten grandchildren. I am her tenth
grandchild, and my name is Lily too!

2 🌐 **2.74 Listen to Lily talking about her early years. Are the sentences true or false?**

a) She was born in Dublin. *False.*

b) Her father was a doctor.

c) She started school when she was seven.

d) The school had one teacher.

e) She married Mr O'Sullivan.

f) Her husband was twenty-six when they got married.

Correct the false sentences.

3 Complete the information about Lily from the text and the listening.

a) Lily was born on *6th May 1922* in *Ireland*.

b) She lived in a very _____ house.

c) She _____ _____ brothers and sisters.

d) She started school when she was _____ .

e) She _____ school and books.

Write similar sentences about your early years. Write one false sentence.

I was born on 10th March 1988 in Madrid, Spain.

Tell your partner about your early years. Can your partner guess the false sentence?

Writing & Speaking

1 Match the beginnings and endings with *when* to make sentences about Lily Byrne on page 92.

a) – 5 She started school when she was seven.

a) She started school   1   she was forty-five.
b) She started university   2   she was forty.
c) She got married   3   she was sixteen.
d) She graduated from   4   she was twenty.
    university   5   she was seven.
e) She started work on
    the farm

2 Complete the sentences about yourself.

a) I started school when I was ...
b) I met my best friend when ...
c) I got my first bicycle / car / mobile phone ...

3 Complete *An interesting life* about a person you know.

> **An interesting life** – _____ (*name*)
>
> He/She was born on _____ in _____ (*place*).
>
> He/She went to school/university in _____ (*place*) in _____ (*year*).
>
> He/She became a _____ in _____ (*year*).
>
> He/She got married to _____ in _____ (*year*).
>
> He/She had _____ children.
>
> Now he/she _____ .

Tell your partner about the person.

4 Write a short description of the person. Use *when he/she was* + age where possible.

> My grandfather, Paolo, is amazing!
> He was born on 20th May 1930
> in Naples.

Birth

School

University

Work

Marriage

Retirement

🎵 2.75 **Song:** *What A Wonderful World*

13 Travel

Grammar Past simple: negative and question forms. *Wh* questions
Vocabulary Travel phrases. Time expressions. *ago*. Holidays
Useful phrases At a railway station

Vocabulary

Travel phrases

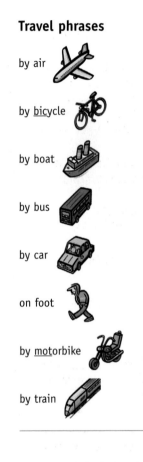

by air

by <u>bi</u>cycle

by boat

by bus

by car

on foot

by <u>mo</u>torbike

by train

1 🌐 3.01 **Listen and repeat the travel phrases.**

2 🌐 3.02 **Listen to travel noises (*1–8*) and write down the appropriate travel phrases.**
1 – by motorbike

3 | Pairwork | **Student A:** page 120 **Student B:** page 125

Reading & Writing

1 **Complete the information below with the correct travel phrases.**

Round the world!

How?
a) _____

How long?
312 days and one hour

Who?
Robin Knox-Johnston (Britain) –
48,197 kilometres in the *Suhaili*

When?
14ᵗʰ June 1968 to 22ⁿᵈ April 1969

How?
b) _____

How long?
69 days 19 hours 5 minutes

Who?
Mohammed and Neena Salahuddin
Choudhury (India) – 40,750 kilometres
in a Hindustan Contessa Classic

When?
9ᵗʰ September to 17ᵗʰ November 1989

2 **Complete the text with the information in Exercise 1.**

> Robin Knox-Johnston went round the world (1) *by boat*. He travelled (2) _____
> kilometres. The journey took 312 (3) _____ and one (4) _____ . He started the
> journey on 14ᵗʰ (5) _____ 1968 and finished on 22ⁿᵈ (6) _____ 1969.

🌐 3.03 **Listen and check.**

3 **Write a similar text about Mohammed and Neena in Exercise 1.**

Reading

1 🌐 **3.04 Read the article. Tick (✓) the places that Ewan and Charlie visited.**

Alaska ☐	Australia ☐	Britain ☐	Canada ☐	Italy ☐	Kazakhstan ☐
Mongolia ☐	Russia ☐	Siberia ☐	Spain ☐	Ukraine ✓	the USA ☐

The **long way** round

From mid-April to the end of July 2004, actors Ewan McGregor and Charlie Boorman went from London to New York by motorbike.

They left London on 14ᵗʰ April and travelled 30,395 kilometres through central Europe, Ukraine, Russia, Kazakhstan, Mongolia, Siberia and Canada.

5   In Siberia there were no roads for part of the journey, so they travelled 933 kilometres by train. They went by air from Magadan in Siberia to Anchorage in Alaska and continued their journey across Canada and the USA. They arrived in New York on 29ᵗʰ July.

Ewan and Charlie are Hollywood stars, but they didn't stay in 5-star hotels.
10 At night, they camped or stayed in motels. Sometimes people invited them into their homes.

They wanted to work with a children's charity, so they visited UNICEF projects in Ukraine, Kazakhstan and Mongolia. They met a lot of children there and made friends for life.

15   After the trip they sold their motorbikes for charity and started planning their next trip.

2 Complete the summary.

(1) *Ewan McGregor* and Charlie Boorman went round the world by (2) _____ . They travelled (3) _____ kilometres. It took (4) _____ and a half months. They started the journey on 14ᵗʰ (5) _____ 2004 and finished on 29ᵗʰ (6) _____ 2004.

🌐 **3.05 Listen and check.**

3 What was the last big journey you did? Tell your partner.

> In 2006 I went to Florida. I went by air and ...

Grammar

Past simple

They **went** by motorbike.
They **didn't stay** in hotels.

Did you **go** by bus?
Yes, I **did**.
No, I **didn't**.

1 Complete the questions and answers about the article on page 95.

a) '*Did* they go round the world by motorbike?'   '*Yes, they did.*'   '*No, they didn't.*'

b) '_____ they leave London on 14ᵗʰ May 2004?'   'Yes, they _____ .' 'No, they _____ .'

c) '_____ they travel by car in Siberia?'   '_____'   '_____'

d) '_____ they arrive in New York on 29ᵗʰ July 2004?' '_____'   '_____'

e) '_____ they meet a lot of children?'   '_____'   '_____'

f) '_____ they sell their motorbikes?'   '_____'   '_____'

🌐 3.06 **Listen, check and repeat.**

2 Work with a partner. Ask and answer the questions in Exercise 1.

3 Complete the table to make it true for today.

Use *in* or *last*	Use *ago*
a) last week =	*a* week ago
b) last *month* =	a month ago
c) in 2002 =	_____ years ago
d) in _____ =	ten years ago
e) last Saturday =	_____ days ago
f) in February =	_____ month(s) ago

4 Say a time expression with *in* or *last*. Your partner says an equivalent expression with *ago*.

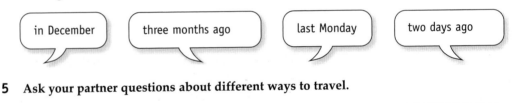

in December   three months ago   last Monday   two days ago

5 Ask your partner questions about different ways to travel.

When was the last time you travelled by taxi?   Last month.   Where did you go?

6 Grammar *Extra* 13 page 134. Read the explanation and do the exercises.

Vocabulary

1 🌐 3.07 **Listen and repeat the words and phrases.**

| bars   a beach   a big ho<u>tel</u>   cold <u>wea</u>ther   <u>discos</u>   the <u>family</u>   friends |
| hot <u>wea</u>ther   <u>moun</u>tains   <u>restau</u>rants   sharks   shops   <u>sight</u>seeing |
| sports   <u>sun</u>bathing   a <u>swimm</u>ing pool   a tent |

2 Put the words and phrases in Exercise 1 in a list below.

A good holiday for me …	A bad holiday for me …
a beach	*cold weather*

Compare your lists with a partner.

Pronunciation

1 **Say the words.**

a) what   hot   lot   <u>hat</u>

b) where   hair   here   wear

c) who   know   true   blue

d) how   show   go   though

e) why   buy   way   high

f) when   ten   bean   men

2 <u>Underline</u> the word with a different sound in each group in Exercise 1.

🌐 **3.08** **Listen, check and repeat.**

Grammar

Wh questions

Wh	subject	verb
Where did	you	go?
What did	he	do?
How did	they	travel?

1 **Write questions about a holiday. Put the subject *you* in the correct position.**

a) Where   did   go ?   *Where did you go?*

b) Why   did   go   there ?

c) When   did   go ?

d) Who   did   go   with ?

e) How   did   travel ?

f) What   did   do ?

🌐 **3.09** **Listen, check and repeat.**

2 **Match the answers in the box with the questions in Exercise 1.**

> 1 By air.   2 Will and Harry.   3 In July.   4 To Ibiza.
>
> 5 We swam and went clubbing.   6 Because the hotel was cheap.

a)   *Where did you go? 4 To Ibiza.*

🌐 **3.10** **Listen to the conversation, and check.**

3 **Ask your partner about their last holiday. Use the questions in Exercise 1.**

Listening & Speaking

1 🌐 **3.11** **A man is talking about his best holiday. Read the questions and listen.** <u>Underline</u> **the answers he gives.**

a) 'Where was your best holiday?' 'My best holiday was in **Paris** / <u>**the Maldives**</u>.'

b) 'When did you go there?' 'It was **last December** / **three years ago**.'

c) 'Who did you go with?' 'I went with **my wife** / **five friends**.'

d) 'How did you travel?' 'We went **by air** / **by boat**.'

e) 'Where did you stay?' 'We stayed **in a tent** / **in a house near the beach**.'

f) 'What did you do?' 'We went **swimming with sharks** / **sightseeing**.'

g) 'How long did you stay?' 'We stayed for **a week** / <u>**two weeks**</u>.'

2 **You are going to tell your partner about your best holiday.**

- Ask yourself the questions in Exercise 1.

- Think about *what* to say and *how* to say it.

- Tell your partner about your best holiday.

Travel

Useful phrases

1 🌐 **3.12 Read, listen and complete the conversation with the numbers in the box.**

| 8.51 | 12.25 | 9.03 | 12 |

Woman: Can I help you?

Man: Yes. Can I have some information about the next train to Paris, please?

Woman: The next train to Paris? OK.

Man: What time does it leave?

Woman: It leaves at (1) _____ .

Man: And what time does it arrive in Paris?

Woman: It arrives in Paris at (2) _____ , local time.

Man: Which platform is it?

Woman: It goes from platform number (3) _____ .

Man: What time is it now, please?

Woman: The time now? It's (4) _____ , sir.

Man: Can I buy a ticket, please?

Woman: A ticket? Yes, over there at the ticket office, sir.

Man: Oh, dear!

Listen and check.

2 🌐 **3.13 Listen and repeat the useful phrases.**
a) Can I have some information about the next train to Paris, please?
b) What time does it leave?
c) What time does it arrive?
d) Which platform is it?
e) Can I buy a ticket, please?

3 Work with a partner. Write a similar conversation about the next train to Brussels. Use the information below.

Practise the conversation.

Time now **16:12**

London to Brussels

Leaves London   **16:35**
Arrives Brussels   **20:35** local time
Platform number   **15**

Vocabulary *Extra*

Holidays

Match the pictures with the words and expressions.

[6] by air

[ ] by boat

[ ] by bus

[ ] by car

[ ] by <u>mo</u>torbike

[ ] by train

[ ] cold <u>weather</u>

[ ] a <u>moun</u>tain

[ ] on foot

[ ] a road

[ ] <u>sight</u>seeing

[ ] <u>sun</u>bathing

[ ] a <u>swim</u>ming pool

[ ] a tent

14 Circus

Grammar *can/can't* for ability. *How many ...?*
Vocabulary Parts of the body. Illness
Useful phrases Talking about illness

▲ circus owner

Reading

1 🔘 3.14 **Read the article. Match the names of the performers. (*a–f*) with their photos (1–6).**

a) Nell b) Gerald c) Nancy d) Tweedy
e) the Kenyan Boys f) Oleg

GIFFORD'S CIRCUS

Nell Gifford started her family circus in 2000. It's a traditional circus of the 1930s – there are no lions or elephants, only horses. Every summer, Gifford's Circus travels round small villages in England.

5 **WHO'S WHO AT GIFFORD'S CIRCUS**

Nell Gifford is the owner of the circus. She joined a circus for a year when she was 18. Then she studied English literature at Oxford University. She performs on her Palomino horse.

10 Gerald can't do any circus tricks, but he's the ring-master at Gifford's Circus.

Nancy is a dancer and performer. She can dance and sing and she loves the life of the circus.

Tweedy is a modern clown – children and adults

15 love him.

It's an international circus. For example, the acrobats, the Kenyan Boys, are from Africa, and the strongman, Oleg, is Russian. Oleg can lift 150 kilogrammes.

▲ acrobats

▲ dancer

2 **Read the article again. Are the sentences true or false?**

a) Gifford's Circus started in 1930.
b) Gifford's Circus travels around England.
c) Nell Gifford went to Oxford University.
d) Gerald is the name of Nell's horse.
e) Nancy loves being in a circus.
f) All the performers are from England.

Correct the false sentences.

3 **When was the last time you went to a circus? Tell your partner.**

> The last time I went to a circus was five years ago. It was great!

▲ strongman

▲ clown

◀ ring-master

Grammar

can / can't

I
You
He
She **can**   dance.
It   **can't** play the piano.
We   speak English.
They

Can you swim?
Yes, I **can**.
No, I **can't**.
can**'t** = can**not**

1 **Complete the questions and answers about Gifford's Circus.**

a) '*Can* Nell Gifford perform on a horse?' 'Yes, she *can* .' 'No, she *can't*.'

b) '_____ Gerald do circus tricks?'   'Yes, he _____ .' 'No, he _____ .'

c) '_____ Nancy dance and sing?'   '_____ .'   '_____ .'

d) '_____ the Kenyan Boys do acrobatics?' '_____ .'   '_____ .'

e) '_____ Oleg lift 150 kilogrammes?'   '_____ .'   '_____ .'

🌐 **3.15** **Listen, check and repeat.**

2 **Look at the article on page 100. Answer the questions.**

3 **What do you know about animals? Complete the following facts with *can* or *can't*.**

a) Cats see in the dark. *Cats **can** see in the dark.*

b) Lions run long distances.

c) Horses sleep on their feet.

d) Lions swim.

e) Horses see colours.

f) Elephants jump.

🌐 **3.16** **Listen, check and repeat.**

4 Grammar *Extra* 14 page 134. Read the explanation and do the exercises.

Pronunciation

🌐 **3.17** **Listen for *can* (/æ/) or *can't* (/ɑː/). Tick (✓) the sentence you hear.**

a) ✓ Jim can swim. ☐ Jim can't swim.

b) ☐ Lance can dance. ☐ Lance can't dance.

c) ☐ Clive can drive. ☐ Clive can't drive.

d) ☐ Lee can ski. ☐ Lee can't ski.

e) ☐ Dell can spell. ☐ Dell can't spell.

f) ☐ Dwight can write. ☐ Dwight can't write.

Listen again and repeat.

Speaking & Writing

1 **Do a survey about class talents.**

- Choose a talent – for example: *play the piano.*
- Write a question with *can* – for example: *Can you play the piano?*
- Ask everybody your question and record the answers – for example: *play the piano?*
  Yes ✓✓✓✓✓ No ✗✗

Class talents

How many people can ...

cook an omelette?   draw?   ride a horse?

play the piano?   type?   ride a motorbike?

Language toolbox

12/12 = everybody

8/12 = most people

4/12 = a few people

0/12 = nobody

2 **Report the results of the survey.**

> Six people can play the piano.
> Two people can't play the piano.

Write a paragraph about your class.

In our class everybody can type, but only one person can ride a motorbike. Eight people can draw, but nobody can ride a horse. A few people can ...

Grammar

How many ...?

How many days are there in a week?

Seven.

1 **Write questions with *How many ...?***

a) players / in a basketball team?
How many players are there in a basketball team?

b) letters / in the English alphabet?

c) strings / on a violin?

d) days / in September?

e) states / in the USA?

f) sports / in a decathlon?

🌐 **3.18 Listen, check and repeat.**

2 **Work with a partner. Ask and answer the questions in Exercise 1.**

🌐 **3.19 Listen and check your answers.**

3 Pairwork **Student A:** page 120 **Student B:** page 125

Vocabulary

1 🌐 **3.20 Listen and repeat the parts of the body.**

2 🌐 **3.21 Listen and do the actions.**

3 **Tell your partner to do some actions.**

Touch your nose.

Circus   U N I T **14**   **103**

Useful phrases

1 Complete the conversations with the words in the box.

| backache | ~~headache~~ | stomach ache | toothache |

a

Alan: What's the matter?
Bella: I have a *headache*.
Alan: Oh, dear. Take an aspirin.
Bella: Yes, good idea!

b

Carole: What's the matter?
Dean: I have _____ .
Carole: Oh, dear. Go to the dentist.
Dean: No, thanks. Do you have an aspirin?

c

Ed: What's the matter?
Fiona: I have _____ .
Ed: Oh, dear. Go to the doctor.
Fiona: Yes, good idea.

d

Greta: What's the matter?
Harry: I have _____ .
Greta: Oh, dear. Where did you have lunch?
Harry: At *Fast Burger*.
Greta: Ah.

🔘 **3.22 Listen and check.**

2 🔘 **3.23 Listen and repeat the useful phrases.**

a) What's the matter?
b) I have a headache.
c) I have toothache.
d) I have backache.
e) I have stomach ache.

f) Oh, dear.
g) Take an aspirin.
h) Go to the dentist.
i) Go to the doctor.
j) Yes, good idea.

3 Work with a partner. Practise the conversations in Exercise 1.

Vocabulary *Extra*

Body

Match the pictures with the words.

- `8` arm
- ☐ back
- ☐ ear
- ☐ eye
- ☐ foot
- ☐ hand
- ☐ head
- ☐ leg
- ☐ mouth
- ☐ nose
- ☐ <u>stom</u>ach
- ☐ tooth

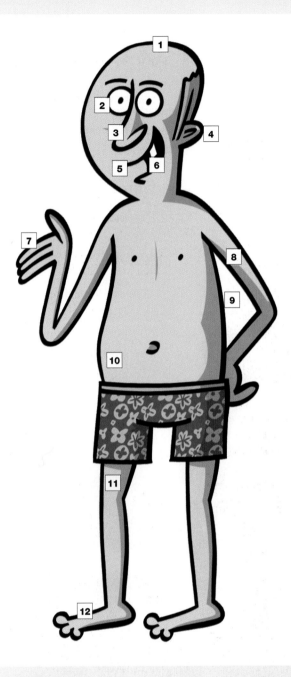

Illness

Match the pictures with the words.

- `2` backache
- ☐ headache
- ☐ stomach ache
- ☐ toothache

15 Future

Grammar *would like to*. Future: *(be) going to*
Vocabulary Time expressions: *next*
Useful phrases Saying goodbye

Reading & Speaking

1 🌐 3.24 **Read the ten things to do before you die.**
Tick (✓) the things you'd like to do. Put a cross (✗) by the things you wouldn't like to do.

Ten things to do before you die
I'd like to …

1	do a bungee jump. ✓	6	go to Machu Picchu. ☐
2	learn to dance the tango. ☐	7	climb Mount Everest. ☐
3	read *The Lord of the Rings*. ☐	8	live in New York. ☐
4	see the Taj Mahal. ☐	9	buy a sports car. ☐
5	meet the Pope. ☐	10	visit the Pyramids. ☐

2 **Use verbs in Exercise 1 to write your own list.**

I'd like to read …   I'd like to see …   I'd like to visit …

Compare your list with a partner. Are you similar or different?

Grammar

would like to

Would you **like to** live
in New York?

Yes, I **would**.
No, I **wouldn't**.

I'd = I **would**

He **wouldn't** =
He **would not**

---

1 Complete the table with *Do you like ...* or *Would you like to ...*

Question 1: _____	Question 2: _____
a) cold weather?	visit Iceland?
b) extreme sports?	do a bungee jump?
c) fast cars?	drive a Ferrari?
d) Shakespeare?	see *Hamlet* at the Globe theatre in London?
e) the British Royal family?	meet the Queen?
f) travelling?	go round the world?
Answer	**Answer**
✓ = Yes, I do.	✓ = Yes, I would.
✗ = No, I don't.	✗ = No, I wouldn't.

🌐 **3.25** Listen, check and repeat the questions and answers.

2 Work with a partner. Ask and answer the questions in Exerise 1.

3 <u>Underline</u> the correct form.

a) I **like** / **'d like to** go to the Moon.

b) My mother **likes** / **would like to** driving.

c) I **don't like** / **wouldn't like to** be famous.

d) My father **doesn't like** / **wouldn't like to** wine.

e) I **like** / **'d like to** learn to dance salsa.

f) I **like** / **'d like to** live in Canada.

🌐 **3.26** Listen, check and repeat.

How many sentences are true for you?

Compare with a partner.

Vocabulary

1 Answer the questions.

a) What time is it now?

b) What day is it today?

c) What day is it tomorrow?

d) What date is it next Saturday?

e) What month is it next month?

f) What year is it next year?

2 🌐 **3.27** Listen and repeat the questions
about the future.

a) When is your next birthday?

b) When is your next dentist appointment?

c) When is your next English lesson?

d) When is your next holiday?

e) When is your next trip abroad?

3 Work with a partner. Ask and answer
the questions in Exercise 2.

Reading & Speaking

1 🌐 **3.28 Read and complete the questionnaire.**

Do you know
your future?

Read and answer the questions with a tick (✓) or a cross (✗).
Read the key. Do you agree?

	✓ = I know	✗ = I don't know

a) What are you going to do this evening?

b) What time are you going to get up tomorrow?

c) Where are you going to have lunch tomorrow?

d) What are you going to do next weekend?

e) What are you going to do for your next birthday?

f) Where are you going to go for your next holiday?

g) Where are you going to be next New Year's Eve?

h) Where are you going to be in 2020?

Key

Mostly ✓ = You're organised. You like planning. You like to be in control.

Mostly ✗ = You're spontaneous. You don't like planning. You live in the present.

2 Compare your answers with a partner.

Grammar

Future: (be) going to

Are you **going to** go out?

Yes, I **am**.

No, I**'m not**.

1 Complete the questions and answers.

After the lesson …

a) '*Are* you *going to* go shopping?'   'Yes, *I am.*'   'No, *I'm not.*'

b) '_____ you going to meet a friend?'   'Yes, _____ .'   'No, _____ .'

c) '_____ going to drive home?'   '_____'   '_____'

d) '_____ to go back to work?'   '_____'   '_____'

e) '_____ phone your friends?'   '_____'   '_____'

f) '_____ have a coffee?'   '_____'   '_____'

🌐 **3.29 Listen, check and repeat.**

2 Work with a partner. Ask and answer the questions in Exercise 1, and say *I don't know* if appropriate.

3 Pairwork **Student A:** page 120 **Student B:** page 125

4 Grammar *Extra* 15 page 134. Read the explanation and do the exercises.

 UNIT 15 **Future**

Pronunciation

1 🌐 **3.30 Listen and repeat chant A.**

A
WHO are you going to TELL?
WHEN are you going to TELL him?
WHY are you going to TELL him?
WHAT'S he going to SAY?

2 **Complete chants B and C.**

B
WHO _____ you going _____ SEE?
WHEN _____ going _____ SEE them?
WHY _____ going _____ SEE them?
WHAT _____ they going _____ SAY?

C
WHO _____ you _____ MEET?
WHEN _____ MEET her?
WHY _____ MEET _____?
WHAT'S _____ SAY?

🌐 **3.31 Listen, check and repeat. Practise the chants.**

Listening & Speaking

1 🌐 **3.32 Listen to an interview with lottery winners, Justin and Kelly, and read the interviewer's questions below.**

Put a tick (✓) if Justin and Kelly give the same answer.
Put a cross (✗) if Justin and Kelly give a different answer.

a) How are you going to celebrate? ✗
b) Where are you going to go on holiday?
c) Where are you going to buy a new house?
d) Who are you going to give money to?
e) Are you going to be happy?

2 **Imagine you are a lottery winner. You have €10 million.**

- Ask yourself the questions in Exercise 1 and make some plans for the future.
- Tell your partner about your plans for the future.

I'm going to go round the world ...

Useful phrases

1   🌐 **3.33 Read, listen and match the conversation with picture *a*, *b* or *c*.**

Tim: Bye, Mum. See you in September.
Mum: Goodbye, Tim. Have a good trip.
Tim: Thanks!
Mum: Phone me when you arrive.
Tim: Yes, of course.
Mum: Take care!
Tim: OK. See you, Mum.
Mum: I love you.
Tim: Yes, I love you, too.
Mum: Write to us, OK?
Tim: Yes, Mum.
Mum: And send us some photos.
Tim: OK.
Mum: Don't forget.
Tim: No, Mum. See you soon. Bye.
Mum: Goodbye, Tim. ... Take care!

2   🌐 **3.34 Read, listen and complete conversations *a* and *b*.**

good	holiday	Monday	See	week

a)   Ann: Bye. See you next (1) _____ .
     Bob: Bye! Have a good (2) _____ .
     Cathy: Thanks.
     Bob: Send us a postcard.
     Cathy: Yes, OK! (3) _____ you soon.

b)   Ms Smith: Goodbye, Mr Jones. See you on (4) _____ .
     Mr Jones: Goodbye, Ms Smith. Have a (5) _____ weekend.
     Ms Smith: Thanks. And you.

3   🌐 **3.35 Listen and repeat the useful phrases.**

a)   See you.
b)   See you soon.
c)   See you in September.
d)   Have a good trip.
e)   Thanks. And you.
f)   Take care!

4   Work with a partner. Practise the conversations in Exercises 1 and 2.

Vocabulary *Extra*

Useful phrases: revision

1 Match the sentences with the pictures.

a) How much are these? 6

b) This is John. ☐

c) Can I speak to Mr Brown, please? ☐

d) What time is it in London? ☐

e) Excuse me. Is there a bank near here? ☐

f) Would you like a cup of tea? ☐

g) Can I have a cappuccino, please? ☐

h) Can I help you? ☐

i) It's my English exam today. ☐

j) What's the matter? ☐

2 Match the sentences (*a–j*) in Exercise 1 with the responses below.

☐ 1 No, thanks.

☐ 2 Er, yes – over there.

☐ 3 I have toothache.

☐ 4 Nice to meet you.

☐ 5 It's 9.30 in the morning.

☐ 6 Oh, good luck!

☐ 7 Small, medium or large?

a 8 Twenty euros.

☐ 9 Yes, I'm looking for a tie.

☐ 10 I'm sorry. He's out.

🌀 3.36 **Listen, check and repeat the conversations.**

3 Work with a partner. Practise three of the conversations.

Review E

Grammar

▶ Grammar *Extra* pages 134 and 135

1 Look at the pictures and complete the sentences about Tina and Bob's weekend away. Use the verbs in the box in the correct form.

| ~~go~~ | go | not like | make | not see | stay |
| travel | visit | not want | | | |

a) Tina and Bob *went* to Scotland. They _____ by train.

b) They _____ in a hotel.

c) They _____ the food.

d) They _____ Loch Ness. They _____ the monster.

e) They _____ to a pub.

f) They _____ some new friends. They _____ to leave.

2 Make questions about Tina and Bob's weekend.

a) travel / by plane? *Did they travel by plane?*

b) stay / in a tent?

c) like / the food?

d) see / the monster

e) go / to a disco?

f) make / some new friends?

g) want / leave?

Answer the questions.

a) *No, they didn't. They travelled by train.*

3 Complete the questions with the words in the box.

| How | How many | What | Where | Who |

a) _____ did you go at the weekend?

b) _____ did you eat for dinner last night?

c) _____ did you have dinner with?

d) _____ hours did you sleep last night?

e) _____ did you travel here today?

Ask and answer the questions with a partner.

4 Write questions with *Can you* and the verbs + phrases in the box.

a) cook spaghetti
b) do circus tricks
c) lift thirty kilogrammes
d) play basketball
e) read *The Lord of the Rings* in one day
f) touch your nose with your foot

a) *Can you cook spaghetti?*

Ask and answer the questions with a partner.

5 <u>Underline</u> the correct form.

a) **I'd like to meet** / **I like to meet** Brad Pitt some day.

b) **I'm going to read** / **I'd like to read** more books, but I don't have the time.

c) **I buy** / **I'm going to buy** some new shoes tomorrow.

d) **I'd like to visit** / **I like to visit** Mexico next year.

e) **I'm going to see** / **I'd like to see** U2 in concert tomorrow. I have a ticket.

f) After the lesson tomorrow **I like to have** / **I'm going to have** lunch with my friend.

Tick (✓) the sentences which are true for you.

6 Spot the mistake! Cross out the incorrect sentence, *a* or *b*.

1 a) ~~When you start this book?~~
  b) When did you start this book?

2 a) Did Jan go to Santander by boat?
  b) Jan went to Santander by boat?

3 a) I can swim.
  b) I can to swim.

4 a) You like a drink?
  b) Would you like a drink?

5 a) How many days are there in February?
  b) How many days there are in February?

6 a) I am going to watch TV tonight.
  b) I am going watch TV tonight.

Vocabulary

1 Complete the crossword with the words for parts of the body. What word is in 10?

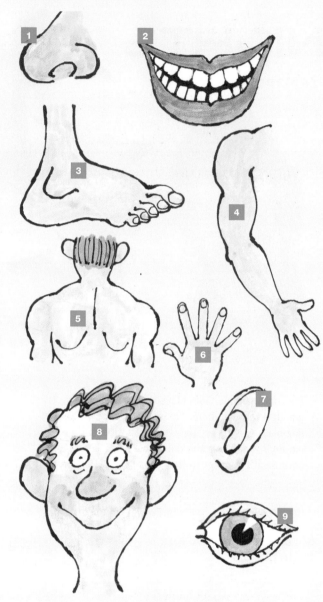

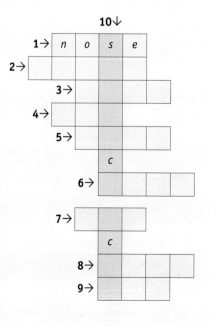

10↓

	1→	n	o	s	e

2→

3→

4→

5→

c

6→

7→

c

8→

9→

2 Complete the travel words.

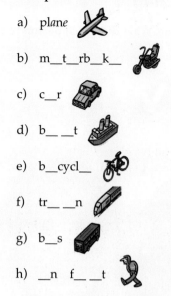

a) pl*ane*

b) m__t__rb__k__

c) c__r

d) b__ __t

e) b__cycl__

f) tr__ __n

g) b__s

h) __n f__ __t

3 <u>Underline</u> the 'odd word out' in each group.

a) mountain   beach   <u>friend</u>

b) shark   bar   disco

c) hotel   weather   shop

d) family   swimming pool   restaurant

e) sport   sightseeing   tent

f) journey   road   trip

4 Complete the time expressions with *ago, in, last* or *next*.

a) I moved here *in* 2004.

b) _____ year I visited friends in England.

c) I learnt to drive two years _____ .

d) I'm going to go shopping _____ Saturday.

e) I always go on holiday _____ August.

f) I started English lessons three months _____ .

g) I didn't do my homework _____ week.

h) I'd like to go to the cinema _____ month.

Rewrite the sentences so that they are true for you.

a) I moved here in 1993.

Compare with a partner.

Pronunciation

1 Look at some words from Units 13–15. Say the words and add them to the table.

<del>ago</del>   arrive   <del>bicycle</del>   <del>birthday</del>   dangerous
holiday   hotel   journey   mountain   nobody
perform   weather

A: ☐ ☐	B: ☐ ☐ ☐	C: ☐ ☐
birthday	*bicycle*	*ago*

2 <u>Underline</u> the stressed syllable in each word.

🔊 3.37 **Listen, check and repeat.**

1 🌐 **3.38 Read the article. What does each person in the band do?**

WHITE NIGHTS
in New Zealand

Tom   Amy   Baz   Olly

British rock band, White Nights, are going to play two concerts here in Wellington on 24th and 25th January. The band are on a four-month tour of the world. The tour started in December and ends in April. Amy sings in the band. She said, 'We're very excited about playing in New Zealand.

It's the first time.' Tom plays the piano. He said, 'My grandparents live here. I'm going to stay with them.' Baz plays the guitar. He would like to visit the Te Papa museum. Olly plays the drums. He said, 'I'm happy because it's summer in New Zealand – in January!'

2 Read the article again. Answer the questions.

a) How many concerts are White Nights going to play in Wellington?

b) How long is the tour?

c) When is the tour going to end?

d) Who has family in New Zealand?

e) What would Baz like to do?

f) Why is Olly happy?

3 Put the word in brackets in the correct place in the questions.

a) How long are you going to in New Zealand ? (stay)

b) Where are you going to after New Zealand ? (go)

c) When did you the tour ? (start)

d) How do you usually ? (travel)

e) What do you all doing when you're not working ? (like)

4 🌐 **3.39 Listen to the interview with Amy. Check the questions you wrote in Exercise 3.**

5 Listen again. Give Amy's answers to the questions in Exercise 3.

a) _____ days.

b) _____ , Australia.

c) _____ weeks ago.

d) Usually by _____ (sometimes by _____).

e) _____ likes sightseeing; _____ likes sports; _____ and I like shopping.

Writing & Speaking

1 Read the announcement. What did you win?

Congratulations!

You're a winner

of a round-the-world trip for two people.
Choose four countries anywhere in the
world – stay for one week in each place.

2 Put the words in the correct order.

a) going to go / are / you / Where ?

b) you / Why / do / want to go there ?

c) you / are / going to travel / How ?

d) are / What / going to do there / you ?

3 Work with a partner. You are going to travel round the world together. Which four countries would you like to visit?

Answer the questions in Exercise 2 for each country.

Country 1: We are going to go to Fiji. We want to go there because it's warm and beautiful. We are going to go by plane to Fiji and then by boat to the islands. We are going to lie on the beach in the day and go to discos at night.

Read your ideas to two other students.

Decide together who chose the best round-the-world tour.

4 Read the email from Olly to his family. Answer the questions.

In which paragraph (*1, 2, 3* or *4*) does Olly write about:

a) the weather and the people?

b) the journey?

c) what he did today?

d) what he's going to do tomorrow?

From: Olly Jones
Date: 20 January
To: Mum and Dad
Subject: We're here!

Dear Mum and Dad

① We're here! We arrived yesterday. The journey took 18 hours, and we didn't sleep – we were so excited!

② It's really hot – it's summer here in New Zealand! We're having a great time – the people are really brilliant.

③ Amy and I went to the beach today. I swam and she read her book. This afternoon we all went sightseeing. Wellington is a beautiful city!

④ We are going to play our first concert tomorrow – very exciting!

Love, Olly xx

5 Write an email from one of the countries you visited on your round-the-world tour.

Write about:
- the journey
- the weather and the people
- what you did today
- what you are going to do tomorrow

Pairwork: Student A

Unit 1 Ask Student B and write the missing names.

_____   Christina   _____   Scarlett   _____   Orlando
Aguilera   Johansson   Bloom

> Number 1. What's his name?   ...   Can you spell that?

Unit 2 Ask Student B and write the missing countries.

a) Claudia Schiffer is from _____ .
b) Julio and Enrique Iglesias are from _____ .
c) JK Rowling is from *Britain*.

d) Bill and Hillary Clinton are from *the USA*.
e) Gisele Bundchen is from _____ .
f) Roman Polanski is from *Poland*.

> Is Claudia Schiffer from the USA?   Are Julio and Enrique Iglesias from Brazil?

Unit 3 The people in the photos are in your family. Invent their names and tell Student B about them.

> This is Rose. She's my mother. This is Bob. He's her boyfriend. He's fifty-three.

Unit 4 Ask Student B questions and complete the list describing the pictures.

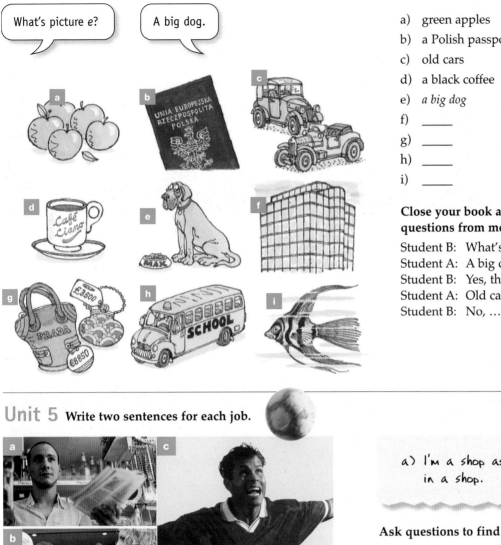

What's picture *e*?

A big dog.

a) green apples
b) a Polish passport
c) old cars
d) a black coffee
e) *a big dog*
f) _____
g) _____
h) _____
i) _____

Close your book and answer Student B's questions from memory.

Student B: What's picture *e*?
Student A: A big dog?
Student B: Yes, that's right. What's picture *g*?
Student A: Old cars?
Student B: No, …

Unit 5 Write two sentences for each job.

a) I'm a shop assistant. I work in a shop.

Ask questions to find out Student B's jobs.

Do you work in an office?
Are you a secretary?

Unit 6 What do you know about Student B?

Write Student B's name in the space below.

<u>Underline</u> the information that you think is true for Student B.

Write questions.

Ask Student B the questions to find out if you are right or wrong.

I think _____ (*Student B's name*) …	Questions	✓ = I'm right! ✗ = I'm wrong!
a) **gets up / doesn't get up** early.	*Do you get up early?*	_____
b) **works / doesn't work** in an office.	_____	_____
c) **has / doesn't have** lunch in a restaurant.	_____	_____
d) **finishes / doesn't finish** work at 5.00 p.m.	_____	_____
e) **goes / doesn't go** shopping on Saturdays.	_____	_____
f) **likes / doesn't like** Sundays.	_____	_____

Unit 7 Don't look at Student B's photo. Ask questions to find out what is similar and what is different about your photos. Use the words in the box or your own ideas.

> buildings   buses   cars   a church   people   a river   shops   a square
> a statue   a street

> **Is there a river in your photo?**
>
> **No, there isn't.**
>
> **Are there any buildings in your photo?**
>
> **Yes, there are.**

Unit 8 Complete the sentences about your home using numbers. Make five true sentences and one false sentence.

a) There are _____ rooms.   c) There are _____ armchairs.   e) There are _____ beds.

b) There are _____ bathrooms.   d) There are _____ sofas.   f) There are _____ televisions.

Exchange sentences with Student B. Guess which of Student B's sentences is false. Write *T* for true or *F* for false.

Check how many sentences Student B guessed correctly.

Unit 9 Read questions *a–e*. Complete question *f* with your own ideas.

Write your answers to the questions in the *Me* column.

Ask Student B the questions and write their answers in the *Student B* column.

Compare your answers. Are you the same or different?

Questions	Me	Student B	Same? Different?
a) How often do you get up early?	_____	_____	_____
b) How often do you have lunch at home?	_____	_____	_____
c) How often do you use the internet?	_____	_____	_____
d) How often do you go out for a meal?	_____	_____	_____
e) How often do you watch television?	_____	_____	_____
f) How often do you _____ ?	_____	_____	_____

Unit 10 Describe one woman to Student B. Say what she's wearing and what she's doing. Student B says which woman you are describing.

Unit 11 Ask Student B questions and complete the information about the famous people.

a) **Ronaldinho**
21st March 1980
Porto Alegre, Brazil

b) **JK Rowling**
_____
Chipping Sodbury, England

c) **Johnny Depp**
9th June 1963
_____

d) **Antonio Banderas**
_____
Malaga, Spain

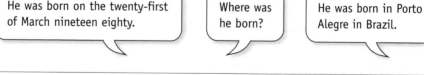

When was Ronaldinho born?

He was born on the twenty-first of March nineteen eighty.

Where was he born?

He was born in Porto Alegre in Brazil.

Unit 12 Read some facts about a sporting hero to Student B. Don't say the person's name! Student B guesses who it is.

> Anna Kournikova   Diego Maradona   Ellen MacArthur   Franz Beckenbauer   George Forman
> Johan Cruyff   Maria Sharapova   'Magic' Johnson   Michael Jordan   Muhammed Ali   Pelé

A
She was born on 8th July 1976.
She bought her first boat when she was eleven.
In 2005 she sailed round the world in 71 days.
Who is it? (*Ellen MacArthur*)

B
He was born on 23rd October 1940.
He won the World Cup in 1958, 1962 and 1970.
He became Minister for Sport in 1994.
Who is it? (*Pelé*)

C
He was born on 17th February 1963.
He won six NBA championships.
He won an Olympic Gold Medal in 1992.
Who is it? (*Michael Jordan*)

Unit 13 What do you know about Student B's travelling habits?

Write Student B's name in the space below.

Complete the sentences with words from box 1 and box 2.

Ask questions to check your answers. Are you right or wrong?

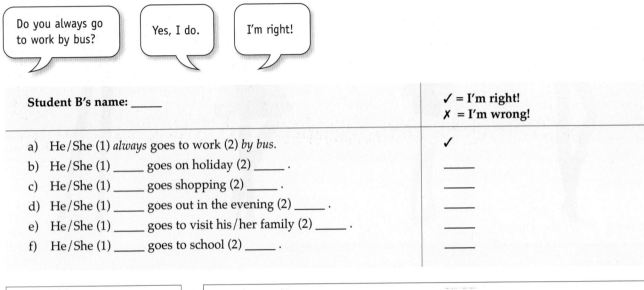

Student B's name: _____	✓ = I'm right! ✗ = I'm wrong!
a) He/She (1) *always* goes to work (2) *by bus*.	✓
b) He/She (1) _____ goes on holiday (2) _____ .	_____
c) He/She (1) _____ goes shopping (2) _____ .	_____
d) He/She (1) _____ goes out in the evening (2) _____ .	_____
e) He/She (1) _____ goes to visit his/her family (2) _____ .	_____
f) He/She (1) _____ goes to school (2) _____ .	_____

1
always   usually sometimes   never

2
by air   by bicycle   by boat   by bus   by car   on foot   by motorbike by train

Unit 14 What do you know about Student B?

Write Student B's name in the space below.

Complete the sentences (*a–f*) with a number.

Write questions to check your answers.

Ask Student B the questions to find out if you are right or wrong.

I think _____ (*Student B's name*) …	Questions	✓ = I'm right! ✗ = I'm wrong!
a) has _____ sisters.	*How many sisters do you have?*	_____
b) has _____ CDs.	_____	_____
c) has _____ jackets.	_____	_____
d) wrote _____ emails yesterday.	_____	_____
e) saw _____ films last month.	_____	_____
f) had _____ holidays last year.	_____	_____

Unit 15 Imagine you are going to do the following actions.

a)   You are going to go skiing.
b)   You are going to go out with your friends.
c)   You are going to ride a horse.
d)   You are going to make a salad.
e)   You are going to do the washing.

Mime each of your preparations.

Student B guesses what you are going to do.

Pairwork: Student B

Unit 1 **Ask Student A and write the missing names.**

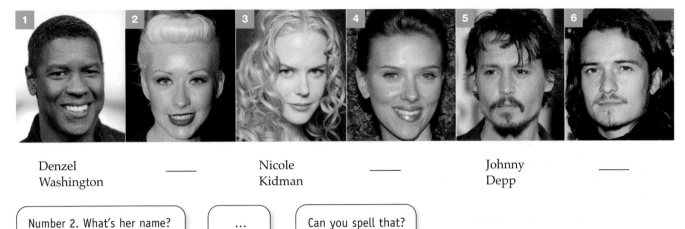

Denzel
Washington

_____

Nicole
Kidman

_____

Johnny
Depp

_____

> Number 2. What's her name?

> ...

> Can you spell that?

Unit 2 **Ask Student A and write the missing countries.**

a) Claudia Schiffer is from *Germany*.

b) Julio and Enrique Iglesias are from *Spain*.

c) JK Rowling is from _____ .

d) Bill and Hillary Clinton are from _____ .

e) Gisele Bundchen is from *Brazil*.

f) Roman Polanski is from _____ .

> Is J K Rowling from the USA?

> Are Bill and Hillary Clinton from the USA?

Unit 3 **The people in the photos are in your family. Invent their names and tell Student A about them.**

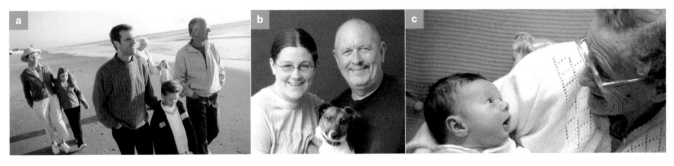

> This is Alan. He's my brother and this is his wife. Her name's Cherie. This is their daughter and her name's Lily. She's ten.

Unit 4 Ask Student A questions and complete the list describing the pictures.

a) _____
b) _____
c) _____
d) _____
e) *a big dog*
f) a new building
g) expensive bags
h) a yellow bus
i) a beautiful fish

Close your book and answer Student A's questions from memory.

Student A: What's picture *e*?
Student B: A big dog?
Student A: Yes, that's right. What's picture *g*?
Student B: Old cars?
Student A: No, …

Unit 5 Write two sentences for each job.

a) I'm a doctor. I work in a hospital.

Ask questions to find out Student A's jobs.

Do you work in an office?
Are you a secretary?

Unit 6 What do you know about Student A?

Write Student A's name in the space below.

<u>Underline</u> the information that you think is true for Student A.

Write questions.

Ask Student A the questions to find out if you are right or wrong.

I think _____ (*Student A's name*) …	Questions	✓ = I'm right! ✗ = I'm wrong!
a) **gets up / doesn't get up** at 7.00 a.m.	*Do you get up at 7.00 a.m?*	_____
b) **works / doesn't work** outside.	_____	_____
c) **has / doesn't have** lunch at home.	_____	_____
d) **finishes / doesn't finish** work at 7.00 p.m.	_____	_____
e) **goes / doesn't go** to the gym on Saturdays.	_____	_____
f) **likes / doesn't like** Mondays.	_____	_____

Unit 7
Don't look at Student A's photo. Ask questions to find out what is similar and what is different about your photos. Use the words in the box or your own ideas.

buildings   buses   cars   a church   people   a river   shops   a square
a statue   a street

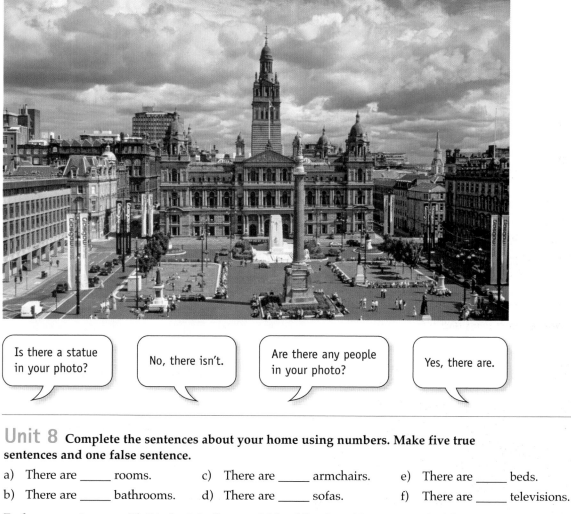

> Is there a statue in your photo?

> No, there isn't.

> Are there any people in your photo?

> Yes, there are.

Unit 8
Complete the sentences about your home using numbers. Make five true sentences and one false sentence.

a) There are _____ rooms.
b) There are _____ bathrooms.
c) There are _____ armchairs.
d) There are _____ sofas.
e) There are _____ beds.
f) There are _____ televisions.

Exchange sentences with Student A. Guess which of Student A's sentences is false. Write *T* for true or *F* for false.

Check how many sentences Student A guessed correctly.

Unit 9
Read questions *a–e*. Complete question *f* with your own ideas.

Write your answers to the questions in the *Me* column.

Ask Student A the questions and write their answers in the *Student A* column.

Compare your answers. Are you the same or different?

Questions	Me	Student A	Same? Different?
a) How often do you get up after 10.00 a.m.?	____	____	____
b) How often do you have eggs for breakfast?	____	____	____
c) How often do you use a cashpoint?	____	____	____
d) How often do you go out for a drink?	____	____	____
e) How often do you listen to the radio?	____	____	____
f) How often do you _____ ?	____	____	____

Unit 10 Describe one woman to Student A. Say what she's wearing and what she's doing. Student A says which woman who you are describing.

a   b   c   d

Unit 11 Ask Student A questions and complete the information about the famous people.

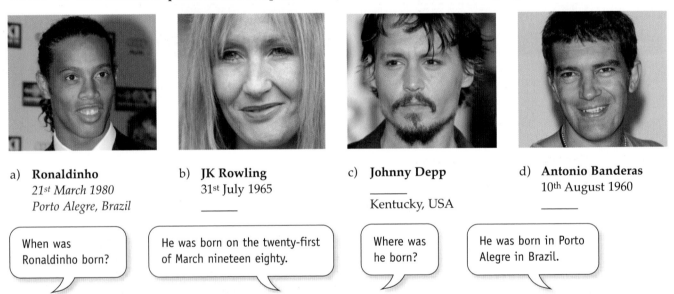

a) **Ronaldinho**
21st March 1980
Porto Alegre, Brazil

b) **JK Rowling**
31st July 1965
_____

c) **Johnny Depp**
_____
Kentucky, USA

d) **Antonio Banderas**
10th August 1960
_____

> When was Ronaldinho born?

> He was born on the twenty-first of March nineteen eighty.

> Where was he born?

> He was born in Porto Alegre in Brazil.

Unit 12 Read some facts about a sporting hero to Student A. Don't say the person's name! Student A guesses who it is.

Anna Kournikova   Diego Maradona   Ellen MacArthur   Franz Beckenbauer   George Forman
Johan Cruyff   Maria Sharapova   'Magic' Johnson   Michael Jordan   Muhammed Ali   Pelé

1
She was born on 19th April 1987.
She became a professional in 2001.
She won Wimbledon in 2004.
Who is it? (*Maria Sharapova*)

2
He was born on 30th October 1960.
He played in Argentina, Spain and Italy.
He became a television presenter in 2005.
Who is it? (*Diego Maradona*)

3
He was born on the 17th January 1942.
He won the world boxing title three times.
He opened the 1996 Olympics in Atlanta.
Who is it? (*Muhammed Ali*)

Unit 13 What do you know about Student A's travelling habits?

Write Student A's name in the space below.

Complete the sentences with words from box 1 and box 2.

Ask questions to check your answers. Are you right or wrong?

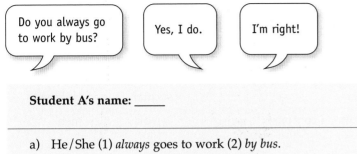

Student A's name: _____	✓ = I'm right! ✗ = I'm wrong!
a) He/She (1) *always* goes to work (2) *by bus*.	✓
b) He/She (1) _____ goes on holiday (2) _____ .	_____
c) He/She (1) _____ goes shopping (2) _____ .	_____
d) He/She (1) _____ goes out in the evening (2) _____ .	_____
e) He/She (1) _____ goes to visit his/her family (2) _____ .	_____
f) He/She (1) _____ goes to school (2) _____ .	_____

1 always usually sometimes never	**2** by air by bicycle by boat by bus by car on foot by motorbike by train

Unit 14 What do you know about Student A?

Write Student A's name in the space below.

Complete the sentences (*a–f*) with a number.

Write questions to check your answers.

Ask Student A the questions to find out if you are right or wrong.

I think _____ (*Student A's name*) …	Questions	✓ = I'm right! ✗ = I'm wrong!
a) has _____ brothers.	*How many brothers do you have?*	_____
b) has _____ televisions.	_____	_____
c) has _____ pairs of jeans.	_____	_____
d) had _____ cups of coffee yesterday.	_____	_____
e) bought _____ DVDs last month.	_____	_____
f) read _____ books last month.	_____	_____

Unit 15 Imagine you are going to do the following actions.

a) You are going to go swimming.
b) You are going to go on a first date.
c) You are going to ride a motorbike.
d) You are going to make an omelette.
e) You are going to do a parachute jump.

Mime each of your preparations.

Student A guesses what you are going to do.

Grammar *Extra*

Unit 1 **Nouns**

Regular forms

Singular	Plural	Spelling
a pen	pens	Add *s*.
a bus	bus**es**	Add *es* after *ch, sh, s, x*.
a dictionary	dictionar**ies**	Delete *y* and add *ies* after a consonant + *y*.

Irregular forms

Singular	Plural
a person	people
a child	children
a man	men
a woman	women

You use *a* with a singular noun. *It's **a** pen.* (NOT ~~It's pen.~~)

⚠ ***a*** **or** ***an*?** You use *a* before a consonant sound: ***a** pen, **a** bus.* You use *an* before a vowel sound: ***an**‿apple, **an**‿exercise.*

this/these

Singular	What's **this?**	It's a **dictionary**.
Plural	What are **these?**	They're **dictionaries**.

You use *this* to refer to a singular noun.
You use *these* to refer to a plural noun.

Unit 2 *be*: **present simple**

Affirmative	Negative
I'**m** You'**re** He'**s**/She'**s**/It'**s** German. We'**re** They'**re**	I'**m not** You **aren't** He/She/It **isn't** Polish. We **aren't** They **aren't**

Question	Answer *Yes*	Answer *No*
Am I **Are** you **Is** he/she/it English? **Are** we **Are** they	Yes, I **am.** Yes, you **are.** Yes, he/she/it **is.** Yes, we **are.** Yes, they **are.**	No, I'**m not.** No, you **aren't.** No, he/she/it **isn't.** No, we **aren't.** No, they **aren't.**

In questions you put *be* before the subject.
Are you English? / Is Pelé Brazilian?
(NOT ~~You are English? / Pele is Brazilian?~~)

Unit 3 **Possessive determiners**

Subject pronoun	Possessive determiner	
I	my	This is **my** family.
you	your	Where are **your** books?
he	his	Charles and **his** wife.
she	her	Camilla and **her** husband.
it	its	What's **its** name?
we	our	This is **our** house.
they	their	We are **their** parents.

You use the same possessive determiner for singular and plural.
***Our** family / **Our** friends* (NOT ~~Ours friends~~)

You use *his* for a man and *her* for a woman.
*Bill and **his** wife = Bill's wife.*

*Hillary and **her** husband = Hillary's husband.*

Possessive *'s* and *s'*

You use *'s* for one person.
My brother's school (= I have one brother.)

You use *s'* for more than one person.
My brothers' school (= I have two brothers.)

Unit 1 **Exercises**

1 Put the words in the correct order.
a) It's / pen / a . *It's a pen.*
b) book / a / It's .
c) a / computer / It's .
d) It's / bus / a .
e) passport / It's / a .
f) dictionary / a / It's .

2 Rewrite the sentences in Exercise 1 in the plural.
a) *They're pens.*

3 Look at the pictures. Write questions and answers.
a) *What's this? It's a bag.*
b) *What are these? They're …*

Unit 2 **Exercises**

1 Write the sentences with contractions.

a) I am from Brazil.
I'm from Brazil.
b) You are from Germany.
c) He is from Italy.
d) She is from Japan.
e) They are from Spain.
f) We are international!

2 Write the sentences in Exercise 1 in the negative.

a) *I'm not from Brazil.*

3 Make questions.

a) The Eiffel Tower is in Moscow.
Is the Eiffel Tower in Moscow?
b) Big Ben is in New York.
c) The Petronas Towers are in Cairo.
d) The Brooklyn Bridge is in London.
e) The Kremlin is in Paris.
f) The Pyramids are in Kuala Lumpur.

4 Answer the questions in Exercise 3.

a) *No, it isn't. It's in Paris.*

Unit 3 **Exercises**

1 Complete the table.

Subject pronoun	Possessive determiner
I	(1) *my*
you	(2) _____
she	her
(3) _____	its
we	(4) _____
they	(5) _____

2 Look at the pictures. <u>Underline</u> the correct form.
a) This is my **parent's** / <u>**parents'**</u> house.
b) This is my **mother's** / **mothers'** car.
c) These are my **father's** / **fathers'** cars.
d) This is my **sister's** / **sisters'** university.
e) These are my **sister's** / **sisters'** boyfriends.
f) These are my **brother's** / **brothers'** girlfriends.

3 Rewrite the sentences in Exercise 2 with *his*, *her* or *their*.

a) *This is <u>their</u> house.*

Unit 4 **Adjectives**

*a **big** house*   *a **small** house*   *an **expensive** car*   *three **expensive** cars*

You use adjectives before a noun. *a **big** house* (NOT ~~a house big~~)
You don't change adjectives before a plural noun. *three **expensive** cars* (NOT ~~three expensives cars~~)

Unit 5 **Present simple:** *I, you, we, they*

Affirmative	Negative
I You We **work.** They	I You We **don't work.** They

Question	Answer *Yes*	Answer *No*
Do I **Do** you **Do** we **work?** **Do** they	Yes, I **do.** Yes, you **do.** Yes, we **do.** Yes, they **do.**	No, I **don't.** No, you **don't.** No, we **don't.** No, they **don't.**

You use *do* to make questions with all verbs for *I, you, we, they*.
You put *do* before the subject. ***Do** you work in a school?* (NOT ~~You work in a school?~~)

You use *don't* to make negative sentences with all verbs for *I, you, we, they*.

Unit 6 **Present simple:** *he, she, it*

Affirmative	Negative
He/She/It **works.**	He/She/It **doesn't work.**

You use *does* to make questions with all verbs for *he, she, it*.
You put *does* before the subject. ***Does** he work in an office?* (NOT ~~He works in an office?~~)

You use *doesn't* to make negative sentences with all verbs for *he, she, it*.

Verb	*he, she, it*	Spelling
live, play, work	lives, plays, works	Add *s*.
watch, finish	watches, finishes	Add *es* after *ch, sh, s, x*.
study	studies	Delete *y* and add *ies* after a consonant + *y*.
do, go, have	does, goes, has	Irregular forms

⚠ *be* You don't use *do* or *does* with *be*. ***Are** you English?* (NOT ~~Do you are English?~~)

Unit 4 **Exercises**

1   **Write the sentences in the plural.**

a)   It's an expensive car.
They're expensive cars.
b)   It's a big city.
c)   It's a Japanese camera.
d)   It's a brown bag.
e)   It's an ugly building.
f)   It's a small hotel.

2   **Put the words in the correct order.**

a)   have / small / a / I / apartment .
I have a small apartment.
b)   a / car / new / have / I .
c)   have / Brazilian / I / a / girlfriend .
d)   big / a / family / I / have .
e)   pen / have / a / I / cheap .
f)   old / an / I / computer / have .

3   **Tick (✓) the sentences in Exercise 2 that are true for you.**

Unit 5 **Exercises**

1   **Write the sentences in the negative.**

a)   I speak Polish.
I don't speak Polish.
b)   I smoke.
c)   I drink beer.
d)   I have a car.
e)   I live with my parents.
f)   I work for my father.
g)   I eat meat.
h)   I like English music.

2   **Tick (✓) the sentences in Exercise 1 that are true for you.**

3   **Put the words in the correct order.**

a)   do / kangaroos / live / Where ?
Where do kangaroos live?
b)   penguins / eat / do / What ?
c)   US Presidents / live / do / Where ?
d)   language / Brazilians / do / speak / What ?
e)   TV programmes / watch / you / do / What ?
f)   study / do / English / you / Where ?

4   **Answer the questions in Exercise 3. Compare with a partner.**

Unit 6 **Exercises**

1   **Write the present simple forms for *he/she/it*.**

a)   do   *does*
b)   finish
c)   get
d)   go
e)   have
f)   like
g)   study
h)   watch

2   **Complete the questions with *Do* or *Does*.**

a)   *Do* you work near your English school?
b)   _____ your lesson finish at 8.00 p.m?
c)   _____ your teacher live near the school?
d)   _____ you watch films in class?
e)   _____ your school have a bar?
f)   _____ you study English at home?

3   **Answer the questions in Exercise 2.**

4   **Pete is a postman. Read about his weekdays. <u>Underline</u> the verbs in the present simple.**

'I <u>get up</u> at 4.30 a.m. I go to work at 5.30 a.m. and I finish work at about 1.00 p.m. I get home at 2.00 p.m. and have lunch at 3.00 p.m. I go to the gym in the afternoon. I have dinner at 7.00 p.m. and I go to bed at about 9.30 p.m.'

5   **Compare your weekdays with Pete's. Write sentences.**

1   *Pete gets up at 4.30 a.m. I get up at 7.00 a.m.*
2   *Pete goes to work …*

Unit 7 *there is / there are; some/any*

	Affirmative	Negative
Singular	**There's** a school.	**There isn't** a hospital.
Plural	**There are** some people.	**There aren't** any bars.

	Question	Answer *Yes*	Answer *No*
Singular	Is there **a doctor**?	Yes, there **is**.	No, there **isn't**.
Plural	Are there **any hotels**?	Yes, there **are**.	No, there **aren't**.

You use *there's* or *there are* to say that something or somebody exists.

With plurals you use *some* in affirmative sentences. *There are **some** people.*

With plurals you use *any* in negative sentences and questions. *There aren't **any** bars.*
*Are there **any** hotels?*

Unit 8 **Object pronouns**

Subject pronoun	Object pronoun	
I	me	He likes **me**.
you	you	I love **you**.
he	him	She hates **him**.
she	her	He hates **her**.
it	it	We don't like **it**.
we	us	Come with **us**.
they	them	Listen to **them**.

You use object pronouns in place of nouns. *This is **John**. I love ~~John~~ **him**.*
You use object pronouns after verbs. *He likes **me**.* (NOT ~~He me likes.~~)

Unit 9 **Adverbs of frequency**

100%   0%

always	usually	sometimes	not usually	never

You use adverbs of frequency before a main verb.
*I **always** have coffee for breakfast.* (NOT ~~I have always coffee …~~)
*He **doesn't usually** drink beer.* (NOT ~~He doesn't drink usually beer.~~)

⚠ **be** You use adverbs of frequency <u>after</u> *be (am / are / is)*. *She's **always** happy.* (NOT ~~She always is happy.~~)

Unit 7 Exercises

1 Match the numbers with the phrases.

a) 7 ─────── minutes in an hour
b) 26 ─────── hours in a day
c) 60 ─────── days in a week
d) 50 ─────── players in a football team
e) 24 ─────── states in the USA
f) 11 ─────── letters in the English alphabet

Write sentences.

a) *There are seven days in a week.*

2 Cross out the incorrect form.

In our classroom …
a) there are ~~any~~ / **some** dictionaries.
b) there's **a** / **an** map of Britain.
c) there are **any** / **some** Italian students.
d) there's **a** / **an** old CD player.
e) there's **a** / **an** computer.
f) there are **any** / **some** photos.

3 Write negative sentences for Exercise 2.

a) *In our classroom there aren't any dictionaries.*

Tick (✓) the sentences in Exercises 2 and 3 that are true for your classroom.

Unit 8 Exercises

1 <u>Underline</u> the correct pronouns.

a) I like her, but <u>she</u> / **her** doesn't like **I** / <u>me</u>.
b) <u>You</u> like **they** / **them**, but **they** / **them** don't like you.
c) He likes **I** / **me**, but I don't like **he** / **him**.
d) **She** / **Her** likes you, but you don't like **she** / **her**.
e) We like **he** / **him**, but he doesn't like **we** / **us**.
f) They like us, but **we** / **us** don't like **they** / **them**.

2 Use the key and write four possible answers to each question.

> **Key**
> ✓✓ = I like him / her / it / them.
> ✗✗ = I don't like him / her / it / them.
> ✓/✗ = He's / She's / It's / They're OK.
> ?? = I don't know him / her / it / them.

a) What do you think of the Beatles?
   I like them.   I don't like them.   <u>They're OK.</u>   I don't know them.
b) What do you think of Brad Pitt?
c) What do you think of Mariah Carey?
d) What do you think of rugby?
e) What do you think of Woody Allen?
f) What do you think of hip hop?

3 <u>Underline</u> appropriate answers for you in Exercise 2.

Unit 9 Exercises

1 Put the words in the correct order.

a) Don – at 7.00 a.m. / gets up / usually
   Don usually gets up at 7.00 a.m.
b) Sue – has / always / a big breakfast
c) Rick – to the gym / sometimes / goes
d) Dana – to school / usually / takes her children
e) Kate – have dinner / doesn't usually / before 8.00 p.m.
f) Jack – goes to bed / before midnight / never

2 Replace the names in Exercise 1 with people you know. Make true sentences.

a) *My mother usually gets up at 7.00 a.m.*

3 Add adverbs of frequency to make sentences that are true for you.

a) I speak English in class.
   I always speak English in class.
b) I use my native language in class.
c) I write down new English words.
d) I use my English dictionary.
e) I study English at home.
f) I read magazines and books in English.

Unit 10 **Present continuous**

Affirmative	Negative
I'm	I'm not
You're	You aren't
He's /She's /It's working.	He/She/It isn't working.
We're	We aren't
They're	They aren't

Spelling
Verbs that end in *e*: *live* ➔ *living*
Verbs that end in one vowel + one consonant:
run ➔ *running*

Question	Answer *Yes*	Answer *No*
Am I	Yes, I am.	No, I'm not.
Are you	Yes, you are.	No, you aren't.
Is he/she/it working?	Yes, he/she/it is.	No, he/she/it isn't.
Are we	Yes, we are.	No, we aren't.
Are they	Yes, they are.	No, they aren't.

You use the present continuous to talk about activities in progress now.

Unit 11 *be*: **past simple**

Affirmative	Negative
I was	I wasn't
You were	You weren't
He/She/It was good.	He/She/It wasn't good.
We were	We weren't
They were	They weren't

You use *was/were* to talk about the past.
*I **was** born in 1960.*
*They **weren't** at home yesterday evening.*
***Was** the film good?*

Question	Answer *Yes*	Answer *No*
Was I	Yes, I was.	No, I wasn't.
Were you	Yes, you were.	No, you weren't.
Was he/she/it good?	Yes, he/she/it was.	No, he/she/it wasn't.
Were we	Yes, we were.	No, we weren't.
Were they	Yes, they were.	No, they weren't.

Unit 12 **Past simple: affirmative forms**

Regular verbs

Verbs	Past simple	Spelling
work, like	work**ed**, lik**ed**	Add *ed*/*d*.
study, try	stud**ied**, tr**ied**	Delete *y* and add *ied* after verbs that end in consonant + *y*.
stop, plan	stop**ped**, plan**ned**	Add consonant + *ed* for verbs that end in one vowel + one consonant.

Irregular verbs: see page 143

You use the past simple to talk about the past.
There is *one* past form for each verb (except *be*: *was/were* – see Unit 11).

*I / You / He / She / It / We / They **worked** yesterday.*
*I / You / He / She / It / We / They **went** to London yesterday.*

Unit 10 Exercises

1 Complete the table.

A	B	C
speak *speaking*	have *having*	sit *sitting*
do _____	make _____	run _____
play _____	write _____	get up _____

2 Write the *ing* form of these verbs and add them to the table.

> come   dance   go   learn   read   sleep   stop
> study   take   work

3 Think about your friends and family. What are they doing now? Write three sentences.

My father's working.

4 Write a question and answer for each picture.

a) *What's he doing?*
    He's running.

Unit 11 Exercises

1 Write affirmative and negative past simple sentences with *be*.

a) I / at home yesterday afternoon.
    I was at home yesterday afternoon.
    I wasn't at home yesterday afternoon.
b) I / in bed at 7.00 a.m. this morning.
c) It / sunny yesterday.
d) *The Simpsons* / on television yesterday evening.
e) My mother / a student in 1978.
f) My parents / born in this country.

2 Tick (✓) the sentences in Exercise 1 that are true for you.

3 Correct the information about these famous people.

a) William Shakespeare was a scientist.
    No, he wasn't. He was a writer.
b) Lady Diana Spencer was born in the USA.
c) Isaac Newton was an actor.
d) Marilyn Monroe was a writer.
e) Pablo Picasso and Salvador Dali were born in France.
f) Christopher Columbus was Spanish.

4 Write three similar sentences for your partner to correct.

1 Elvis Presley was German.

Unit 12 Exercises

1 Complete the table for these regular verbs.

Verb	Past simple
work	(1) *worked*
live	(2) _____
(3) _____	stopped
study	(4) _____
like	(5) _____
complete	(6) _____
(7) _____	tried
(8) _____	listened

2 Complete the sentences in the past simple with these irregular verbs.

a) I *said* my first word when I was two. (say)
b) I _____ my first film at the cinema when I was seven. (see)
c) I _____ my first CD when I was nine. (buy)
d) I _____ my first mobile phone when I was twelve. (get)
e) I _____ abroad for the first time when I was fourteen. (go)
f) I _____ my first English lesson when I was sixteen. (have)

3 Change the ages in Exercise 2 to make the sentences true for you. Then compare with a partner.

Unit 13 Past simple: all forms

Affirmative	Negative
I You He/She/It **worked.** We **went.** They	I You He/She/It **didn't work.** We **didn't go.** They

You use *Did* to make questions with all verbs except *be*.
You put *Did* before the subject.
***Did** you go shopping?* (NOT ~~You went shopping?~~)

You use *didn't* to make negative sentences with all verbs except *be*.

Question	Answer *Yes*	Answer *No*
Did I **Did** you **Did** he/she/it **work?** **Did** we **go?** **Did** they	Yes, I **did.** Yes, you **did.** Yes, he/she/it **did.** Yes, we **did.** Yes, they **did.**	No, I **didn't.** No, you **didn't.** No, he/she/it **didn't.** No, we **didn't.** No, they **didn't.**

⚠ **be** You don't use *did* with *be*.
Were you at work yesterday?
(NOT ~~Did you be at work yesterday?~~)

Unit 14 *can*

Affirmative	Negative
I You He/She/It **can swim.** We **can dance.** They	I You He/She/It **can't swim.** We **can't dance.** They

You use *can* to talk about ability.
You put *can* before the subject in questions.
***Can** you swim?* (NOT ~~You can swim?~~)

Question	Answer *Yes*	Answer *No*
Can I **Can** you **Can** he/she/it swim? **Can** we **Can** they	Yes, I **can.** Yes, you **can.** Yes, he/she/it **can.** Yes, we **can.** Yes, they **can.**	No, I **can't.** No, you **can't.** No, he/she/it **can't.** No, we **can't.** No, they **can't.**

⚠ You don't use *to* after *can*.
I can swim. (NOT ~~I can to swim.~~)

Unit 15 *(be) going to*

Affirmative	Negative
I'm You're He/She/It's **going to** come. We're They're	I'm **not** You **aren't** He/She/It **isn't going to** come. We **aren't** They **aren't**

You use *(be) going to* to talk about your future plans and intentions.

Question	Answer *Yes*	Answer *No*
Am I **Are** you **Is** he/she/it **going to** come? **Are** we **Are** they	Yes, I **am.** Yes, you **are.** Yes, he/she/it **is.** Yes, we **are.** Yes, they **are.**	No, I'm **not.** No, you **aren't.** No he/she/it **isn't.** No, we **aren't.** No, they **aren't.**

Unit 13 **Exercises**

1 Write the sentences in the negative.

a) I had coffee for breakfast.
   I didn't have coffee for breakfast.
b) I went shopping.
c) I did the housework.
d) I watched a film on television.
e) I walked to work.
f) I bought a newspaper.
g) I wrote a letter.
h) I made dinner.

2 Think about yesterday. Tick (✓) the sentences in Exercise 1 that are true for you.

3 Write past simple questions with *you* for the sentences in Exercise 1.

a) *Did you have coffee for breakfast yesterday?*
b) *Did you go shopping yesterday?*
c) *Did you …*

4 Ask your partner the questions in Exercise 3.

Unit 14 **Exercises**

1 Write sentences with *can* and *can't*.

a) I / English / not Japanese (speak)
   I can speak English, but I can't speak Japanese.
b) I / a bicycle / not a horse (ride)
c) I / a car / not a bus (drive)
d) I / the guitar / not the piano (play)
e) I / music / not Chinese (read)
f) I / football / not tennis (play)

2 Rewrite the sentences in Exercise 1 with *and* or *but* so they are all true for you.

I can speak English and I can speak Japanese.

3 Put the words in the correct order.

a) help / you / I / Can ?
   Can I help you?
b) me / you / hear / Can ?
c) dictionary / I / your / Can / use ?
d) door / Can / answer / the / you ?
e) salt / Can / the / you / pass ?
f) cappuccino / have / I / a / Can ?

4 Match the questions (*a–f*) in Exercise 3 with the situations (*1–6*).

a) 1

> 1 in a shop   2 at the dinner table
> 3 on a mobile phone   4 in the classroom
> 5 in a café   6 at home

Unit 15 **Exercises**

1 Write true sentences about tomorrow with *I'm going to* or *I'm not going to*.

a) sell my house
   I'm not going to sell my house tomorrow.
b) get up before 8.00 a.m.
c) drive a car
d) play tennis
e) buy a new mobile phone
f) walk to work

2 Write questions for the sentences in Exercise 1. Then ask your partner.

a) *Are you going to sell your house tomorrow?*

3 Write what these people are going to do this evening.

a) *She's going to watch television.*

Recordings

Unit 1

1.04
(J = Jinx; JB = James Bond)
J: What's your name?
JB: My name's Bond … James Bond.

1.05
(J = Jinx; JB = James Bond)
J: Hello. I'm Jinx. What's your name?
JB: My name's Bond … James Bond.
J: Nice to meet you, James.

1.06
a)   'What's his name?'
     'His name's Pierce Brosnan.'
b)   'What's her name?'
     'Her name's Teri Hatcher.'

1.08
a)   one, two, three, four, five
b)   five, four, three, two, one
c)   two, four, six, eight, ten
d)   one, three, five, seven, nine

1.09
a)   'What's your home number?'
     '020 –7413–6995.'
b)   'What's your mobile number?'
     '07007–856–321.'

1.11
1   'What's this?' 'It's a bag.'
2   'What's this?' 'It's a computer.'
3   'What are these?' 'They're books.'
4   'What are these?' 'They're pens.'
5   'What are these?' 'They're keys.'
6   'What's this?' 'It's a mobile phone.'
7   'What's this?' 'It's a passport.'
8   'What's this?' 'It's a camera.'

1.12
(G = Greg; T = Tina)
G: Hi, Tina.
T: Oh, hi, Greg.
G: What's in your bag?
T: A computer, a camera, three books,
    a mobile phone, er … my passport …
    What's in your bag?
G: A mobile phone.
T: Oh. Where's your computer?
G: In my mobile phone.
T: Where's your camera?
G: In my mobile phone.
T: Where's your passport?
G: Passport? Oh no!

1.14
1   B, C, D, E, G, P, T, V
2   F, L, M, N, S, X, Z
3   A, H, J, K
4   Q, U, W
5   I, Y
6   O
7   R

1.15
1 USA 2 UK 3 VIP 4 OK 5 NYC 6 CIA

Unit 2

1.18
And now on *International Pop Star*,
please welcome …
Number 1 from Italy!
Number 2 from Germany!
Number 3 from Poland!
Number 4 from Japan!
Number 5 from Brazil!
Number 6 from Spain!

1.19
1 Italy   2 Germany
3 Poland
4 Japan   5 Brazil
6 Spain

1.20
a)   'Is Anna from Germany?'
     'Yes, she is.' 'No, she isn't.'
b)   'Is Rosa from Japan?'
     'Yes, she is.' 'No, she isn't'.
c)   'Is Daniel from Poland?'
     'Yes, he is.' 'No, he isn't.'
d)   'Are Roberto and Donna from Brazil?'
     'Yes, they are.' 'No they aren't.'
e)   'Are you from Spain?'
     'Yes, I am.' 'No, I'm not.'
f)   'Are you and your teacher from Italy?'
     'Yes, we are.' 'No, we aren't.'

1.21
a)   'Where are you from?'
     'I'm from Paterna. It's near Valencia
     in Spain.'
b)   'Where are you from?'
     'We're from Niteroi. It's near Rio
     de Janeiro in Brazil.'

1.23
a)   She's Spanish.
b)   It's Polish.
c)   He's British.
d)   They're Italian.
e)   They're Japanese.
f)   They're German.

1.25
a)   twenty-one, twenty-two, twenty-three
b)   thirty-four, thirty-five, thirty-six
c)   forty-seven, forty-eight, forty-nine
d)   one hundred and eleven, one hundred
     and twelve, one hundred and thirteen

1.26
a)   Join thirty, sixty-six and fourteen. Join
     thirteen, thirty and seventy-four.
b)   Join fifteen, fifty and ninety-nine. Join
     fifteen and twenty four. Join fifty and
     eighty-three. Join ninety-nine and one
     hundred and ninety-nine.
c)   Join eighteen, seventy and seventy-
     nine. Join eighteen, eighty and one
     hundred and sixty. Join one hundred
     and sixty, thirty-eight and twenty-nine.

1.28
a)   Three dollars fifty.
b)   Five pounds thirty.
c)   Seventy euros seventy-five.
d)   Nineteen dollars ninety-nine.
e)   Eighty euros twenty.
f)   Forty euros forty.
g)   One hundred and sixteen pounds.

1.29
a)   'How much is a cappuccino in
     New York?'
     'Three dollars.'
b)   'How much is a hamburger in Moscow?'
     'One dollar fifty.'
c)   'How much is a cinema ticket in
     London?'
     'Sixteen dollars fifty.'
d)   'How much is a 3-star hotel in Tokyo?'
     'One hundred and seventy-seven
     dollars.'

1.30
a)   How much is a cappuccino in Rome?
b)   How much is a hamburger in London?
c)   How much is a cinema ticket in Tokyo?
d)   How much is a 3-star hotel in Moscow?

Unit 3

1.33
This is my family and this is me. My name's
Luisa. This is my mum. Her name's Helen.
This is my dad. His name's William. This is
my big brother. His name's Sam, and this is
my baby sister. Her name's Emma. These are
my grandparents. My grandma's name is
Hannah, and my grandpa's name is Tom. Oh,
and this is our dog. His name's Max.

1.35
a)   'How old are you?' 'I'm six.'
b)   'How old is your brother?'
     'He's twelve.'
c)   'How old is your sister?' 'She's one.'
d)   'How old are your mother and father?'
     'They're forty-three.'
e)   'How old is your grandmother?'
     'She's sixty-eight.'
f)   'How old is your grandfather?'
     'He's seventy.'

1.36
a)   Helen is Luisa's mother.
b)   Sam is Luisa's brother.
c)   Tom is Luisa's grandfather.
d)   Emma is Luisa's sister.
e)   William is Luisa's father.
f)   Hannah is Luisa's grandmother.

1.37

(T = Tom; F = Friend)

T: This is in Italy. This is me, and this is my wife.
F: Hannah?
T: Yes, that's Hannah. And this is my daughter getting married.
F: Aah, lovely. What's her name?
T: Helen, and her husband's name is William.
F: And are these your grandchildren?
T: Yes. This is my grandson, Sam.
F: How old is he?
T: He's twelve. And this is Luisa. She's six.
F: And the baby – how old is he?
T: She. That's my granddaughter, Emma. She's one.

1.40

a) John Travolta and his wife are American.
b) Blythe Danner and her children are actors.
c) Jake Paltrow and his sister are actors.
d) John Travolta, Kelly Preston and their two children live in Florida.
e) Jett Travolta says, 'My sister and I are American. Our parents are from the USA.'

1.41

a) I have one sister and one brother.
b) My parents have a dog.
c) My mother has three brothers.
d) My grandparents have two houses.
e) My husband and I have two children.
f) My father has a Japanese car.

1.42

a) He's a teacher. She's an actor.
b) He has a radio. She has an iPod.
c) He has a Fiat. She has an Alfa Romeo.

1.43

an Audi, an English dictionary, an Ericsson mobile phone, an IBM computer, an Italian grandmother
a brother, a dog, a Gucci bag, a passport, a sister

Review A

1.47

A: adjective, Germany, granddaughter, singular
B: computer, description, possessive, relation
C: Japanese, seventeen

1.48

(R = Receptionist;
AS = Arnold Schwarzenegger)

R: Good afternoon, sir.
AS: Good afternoon. How much is one night at this hotel?
R: £85.
AS: Sorry?
R: One night is £85.
AS: Oh, OK. One night, please.
R: What's your first name?
AS: Arnold.
R: Can you spell that?
AS: A–R–N–O–L–D.
R: And your surname?

AS: Schwarzenegger.
R: Sorry. Can you repeat that?
AS: Schwarzenegger.
R: Schwarzenegger? Can you spell that, please?
AS: S–C–H–W–A–R–Z–E–N–E–G–G–E–R.
R: Sorry. Can you repeat that?
AS: S–C–H–W–A–R–Z–E–N–E–G–G–E–R.
R: Are you American, Mr Schwarzenegger?
AS: Yes, I am. I'm from Los Angeles.
R: Do you have a phone number?
AS: Yes, it's 001–310–863–429.
R: Your passport number please, Mr Schwarzenegger.
AS: It's 489–798–2340.
R: Can your repeat that, please?
AS: 489–798–2340.
R: Thank you. Your room number is 103.

Unit 4

1.49

Food: fruit, meat, fish, Italian food, Chinese food
Drink: Coke, wine, coffee, tea
Sport: swimming, tennis, football

1.51

a) 'Do you like Italian food?'
    'Yes, I do.' 'No, I don't.'
b) 'Do you like Chinese food?'
    'Yes, I do.' 'No, I don't.'
c) 'Do you like fish?'
    'Yes, I do.' 'No, I don't.'
d) 'Do you like fruit?'
    'Yes, I do.' 'No, I don't.'
e) 'Do you like coffee?'
    'Yes, I do.' 'No, I don't.'
f) 'Do you like Coke?'
    'Yes, I do.' 'No, I don't.'

1.53

a) What's her favourite city?
b) Who's her favourite actor?
c) Who's her favourite singer?
d) What's her favourite sport?
e) What's her favourite food?
f) What's her favourite drink?

1.55

a) 3 Oxford Street. A red bus, black taxis and expensive shops in London.
b) 1 Red Square. A big square with old buildings in Moscow.
c) 4 Copacabana Beach. Blue sky and beautiful people in Rio de Janeiro.
d) 2 La Boca. Small houses. Red, orange, blue and yellow walls in Buenos Aires.

1.56

beautiful – ugly
big – small
cheap – expensive
new – old

1.58

a) I like black coffee.
b) I like French films.
c) I like old buildings.
d) I like expensive shops.
e) I don't like British food.
f) I don't like big cities.

Unit 5

1.62

a) I live in an old house. I live with my parents.
b) I have one brother. I have an old car.
c) I work in an office. I work for IBM.
d) I like swimming. I like jazz.
e) I speak English. I speak Japanese.
f) I eat meat. I eat fish.

1.63

a) 'Do you speak Chinese?'
    'Yes, I do.' 'No, I don't.'
b) 'Do you smoke?'
    'Yes, I do.' 'No, I don't.'
c) 'Do you and your family live in a city?'
    'Yes, we do.' 'No, we don't.'
d) 'Do your friends like football?'
    'Yes, they do.' 'No, they don't.'
e) 'Do you eat meat?
    'Yes, I do.' 'No, I don't.'
f) 'Do your parents have a dog?'
    'Yes, they do.' 'No, they don't.'

1.64

a) Where do you live?
b) Where do you work?
c) What languages do you speak?
d) What food do you like?
e) What music do you like?
f) What sports do you like?

1.65

a) She's a lawyer.
b) He's a taxi driver.
c) He's a football player.
d) He's a pilot.
e) He's an artist.
f) She's a musician.

1.67

a) I work in a hospital. I'm a doctor.
b) I work in an office. I'm a secretary.
c) I work in a shop. I'm a shop assistant.
d) I work for British Airways. I'm a flight attendant.
e) I work for *Hello* magazine. I'm a journalist.
f) I work outside. I'm a farmer.

1.69

(I: Interviewer; M: Man; W: Woman)

1 I: Excuse me. What do you do?
   W1: I'm a teacher.
   I: What's your dream job?
   W1: Oh, um, musician.
   I: Thank you.

2 I: Excuse me. What do you do?
   M1: I'm a lawyer.
   I: And what's your dream job?
   M1: My dream job? Football player.
   I: Thank you.

3 I: Excuse me. What do you do?
   M2: I'm a taxi driver.
   I: What's your dream job?
   M2: Em, pilot. Yes, pilot.
   I: Thank you.

➡

4 I: Excuse me. What do you do?
   W2: I'm a student.
   I: What's your dream job?
   W2: Oh, I don't know. Em, doctor.
        No, DJ. No, doctor.
   I: Doctor?
   W2: No, DJ.
   I: DJ?
   W2: Yes, DJ.
   I: Thank you.

5 I: Excuse me. What do you do?
   W3: I'm an actor.
   I: What's your dream job?
   W3: My dream job? Actor!
   I: Thank you.

🔊 1.70

a) What do you do?
b) What's your dream job?

Unit 6

🔊 1.73

a) 'What time is it in San Francisco?'
    'It's four o'clock in the morning.'
b) 'What time is it in Buenos Aires?'
    'It's nine o'clock in the morning.'
c) 'What time is it in London?'
    'It's midday, twelve p.m.'
d) 'What time is it in Moscow?'
    'It's three o'clock in the afternoon.'
e) 'What time is it in Hong Kong?'
    'It's eight o'clock in the evening.'
f) 'What time is it in Wellington?'
    'It's midnight, twelve a.m.'

🔊 1.74

a) Four a.m. It's four o'clock in
    the morning.
b) Nine a.m. It's nine o'clock in
    the morning.
c) Twelve p.m. It's midday.
d) Three p.m. It's three o'clock in
    the afternoon.
e) Eight p.m. It's eight o'clock in
    the evening.
f) Twelve a.m. It's midnight.

🔊 1.76

a) It's twelve o'clock.
b) It's five past.
c) It's ten past.
d) It's quarter past.
e) It's twenty past.
f) It's twenty-five past.
g) It's half past.
h) It's twenty-five to.
i) It's twenty to.
j) It's quarter to.
k) It's ten to.
l) It's five to.

🔊 1.77

a) It's two thirty. – It's half past two.
b) It's seven fifty. – It's ten to eight.
c) It's three thirty-five. – It's twenty-five
    to four.
d) It's ten fifteen. – It's quarter past ten.
e) It's five-oh-five. – It's five past five.
f) It's twelve forty-five. – It's quarter
    to one.

🔊 1.80

My day, my night

On weekdays
I get up early, have breakfast and take my
son to school. Then I go to the gym. After
that I go to work in a recording studio.
I finish work at 6.00 p.m. and have dinner
with my family. We have two young
children, Jake and Phoebe, so we go to bed
early.

On Saturdays
I go to bed in the afternoon and then I go
to work in the evening. I work all night in
a club. My favourite club is Gatecrasher
in Liverpool, but I work in clubs all round
the world. Visit my website at
www.judgejules.net for club dates. I work
hard, but I also have a good time.

On Sundays
I get home in the morning, have a shower
and have lunch with my family. In the
afternoon I relax. I listen to music and play
with my children.

🔊 1.81

a) 'Does he go to the gym on weekdays?'
    'Yes, he does.' 'No, he doesn't.'
b) 'Does he have children?'
    'Yes, he does.' 'No, he doesn't.'
c) 'Does he go to bed in the evening
    on Saturdays?'
    'Yes, he does.' 'No, he doesn't.'
d) 'Does he work in clubs all round
    the world?'
    'Yes, he does.' 'No, he doesn't.'
e) 'Does he like his job?'
    'Yes, he does.' 'No, he doesn't.'
f) 'Does he get home in the evening
    on Sundays?'
    'Yes, he does.' 'No, he doesn't.'

🔊 1.85

Good morning. Good afternoon.
Good evening.   a) Hello.

Goodnight.   b) Goodbye.

Review B

🔊 1.86

A: France, gets, smokes
B: taxi, watches, Wednesday
C: Brazil, Madrid, o'clock
D: expensive, musician, relaxes

🔊 1.88

(P = Paula; D = Dan)
P: Hello? Is that Dan Hovey?
D: Yes. Who is this?
P: Hi, I'm Paula Fox. I work for *Blue Jazz*
    music magazine in London.
D: Oh. OK. What time is it in London,
    Paula?
P: Er, it's three o'clock in the afternoon.
D: Well, Paula it's ten o'clock in the
    morning here.
P: Oh … er, sorry, Dan. Look, can I ask
    you some questions for the magazine?
D: Er, yes, OK.
P: Where do you live?
D: Here, in New York.
P: OK. And where do you work?

D: In a jazz club – *The Night Life*.
P: OK. What languages do you speak?
D: Er, English, and Italian. My wife's
    Italian, you see.
P: Oh. And who's your favourite
    musician?
D: Chet Baker.
P: Oh, could you spell that, please?
D: C–H–E–T, B–A–K–E–R.
P: Uh huh. And what's your favourite
    colour?
D: Er, um … red.
P: What's your favourite city? Do you like
    London?
D: Er, yes, I do. But I love New York!
P: Oh. And what's your favourite food?
D: Steak.
P: OK. And finally, what time do you
    get up?
D: 11.30.
P: Oh, yes, sorry! Thank you, Dan.
    Goodbye.
D: Goodbye, Paula.

Unit 7

🔊 2.01

1 The Chrysler Building
2 Grand Central Station
3 Central Park
4 Times Square
5 The Metropolitan Museum
6 Brooklyn Bridge
7 The Statue of Liberty

🔊 2.03

a) 'I love New York. I live in an old
    apartment in the East Village, near the
    university. I work in an office near the
    Hudson river. My favourite place in
    New York is Chinatown – I love
    Chinese food, and there are some
    fantastic restaurants.'
b) 'I love New York and I love Manhattan.
    I live in a small apartment near
    Washington Square Park. I'm a student
    but at the weekend I work in a sports
    shop near the Chrysler Building. My
    favourite place in New York is the
    Hudson Hotel – the cocktails are very
    good.'
c) 'I love New York. I live in an apartment
    in Greenwich Village. I work in a bank
    near Grand Central Station. My
    favourite place in New York is Central
    Park. I love sitting near the lake,
    watching people.'

🔊 2.04

a) There's a zoo.
b) There are 36 bridges.
c) There are three restaurants.
d) There are six cafés.
e) There's a museum.
f) There are 25 million visitors every year.

2.06

a) 'Is there a station near your house?'
'Yes, there is.' 'No, there isn't.'
b) 'Are there any restaurants near your house?'
'Yes, there are.' 'No, there aren't.'
c) 'Is there a museum in your city?'
'Yes, there is.' 'No, there isn't.'
d) 'Is there a park near your house?'
'Yes, there is.' 'No, there isn't.'
e) 'Are there any hotels in your city?'
'Yes, there are.' 'No, there aren't.'
f) 'Is there a church near your house?'
'Yes, there is.' 'No, there isn't.'

2.07

a) a pharmacy; a chemist's
b) an ATM; a cashpoint
c) a subway station; an underground station
d) a restroom; a toilet

Unit 8

2.11

Paul McCartney – the early years

This small house was the home of the McCartney family. Downstairs, there's a hall, a living room, a dining room and a kitchen. Upstairs, there are three bedrooms. Paul's bedroom is the small room above the front door. There's also a bathroom and a toilet. The Beatles wrote their first number one hit *Love Me Do* in the living room. The house is a museum now, and thousands of tourists visit each year.

2.12

This is 20 Forthlin Road in Liverpool, Paul McCartney's family home.
This is the kitchen. There's a washing machine, a sink and a cooker.
This is the dining room. There's a table with six chairs. Can you imagine dinner with the McCartney family in this room? On the walls there are photos of the family. There's a photo of Paul. He's playing his guitar.
This is the living room. There's a television – one of the first. There's an armchair and a sofa. There's also a lamp and an old carpet.
There are three small bedrooms. This is Paul's bedroom. This is his bed and this is his chair.
This is the bathroom. There's a bath, but there isn't a shower. And this is the toilet.

2.13

a) a washing machine
b) a sink
c) a cooker
d) a table
e) chairs
f) a television
g) an armchair
h) a sofa
i) a lamp
j) a carpet
k) a bed
l) a bath
m) a shower
n) a toilet

2.14

a) There's a washing machine in the kitchen.
b) There's a carpet in the living room.
c) There's a bed in Paul's bedroom.
d) There's a sofa in the living room.
e) There's a cooker in the kitchen.
f) There's a television in the living room.

2.16

a) 'What do you think of supermarkets?'
'I like them.' 'I don't like them.'
b) 'What do you think of your house?'
'I like it.' 'I don't like it.'
c) 'What do you think of your city?'
'I like it.' 'I don't like it.'
d) 'What do you think of your neighbours?'
'I like them.' 'I don't like them.'
e) 'What do you think of David Beckham?'
'I like him.' 'I don't like him.'
f) 'What do you think of Hillary Clinton?'
'I like her.' 'I don't like her.'

2.18

a) Mr and Mrs Robinson live on the second floor.
b) Tina Brown lives on the third floor.
c) Mr Taylor lives on the first floor.
d) Robert Turner lives on the fifth floor.
e) The Smiths live on the fourth floor.

Unit 9

2.23

Drinks: beer, coffee, cola, milk, orange juice, tea
Breakfast: bread, cereal, eggs
Lunch/Dinner: chips, fruit, green beans, a hamburger, ice cream, meat, potatoes, salad
Snacks: biscuits, cake, chocolate

2.24

a) 3   Every three hours.
b) 4   Every day.
c) 6   Every morning.
d) 1   Every Saturday.
e) 2   Every week.
f) 5   Never.

2.25

a) How often do you drink coffee?
b) How often do you drink beer?
c) How often do you drink tea?
d) How often do you eat hamburgers?
e) How often do you eat fruit?
f) How often do you eat chocolate?

2.27

a) 2   Mike never cooks at home.
b) 5   Mike sometimes has a cup of coffee for breakfast.
c) 3   Mike always has noodles for dinner.
d) 1   Mike usually drinks beer with his dinner.
e) 4   Mike doesn't usually spend more than $4 a day.

2.29

/ɪ/: drink, fish, chips, milk
/iː/: eat, meat, beans, tea

Review C

2.32

A: biscuit, building, chocolate, minute
B: cereal, possible, Saturday, theatre
C: delicious, fantastic, museum, potato

2.34

(L = Linda; N = Nick)
L: Hello. Nick Sutton?
N: Yes.
L: I'm Linda Sondstrum.
N: Ah, Linda. Thanks for coming in. Would you like a cup of coffee?
L: Er, can I have cup of tea, please? Sorry, I don't really like coffee.
N: Of course. Now, I think I have a place for you. It's a third-floor apartment in Manhattan.
L: Great!
N: There are two bedrooms and two bathrooms. One room has a bath. The other room has a shower.
L: OK.
N: There's a large kitchen with a new cooker.
L: Fantastic!
N: And it's very near Central Park!
L: Oh, that's wonderful.
N: Grand Central Station is only ten minutes away. Oh, and there are lots of really good restaurants and cafés, near the apartment. What do you think?
L: I love it! … Now, how much is it?
N: OK, well, it is in a fantastic location …

Unit 10

2.35

a)
1 a black jacket   3 blue trousers
2 a yellow T-shirt   4 black shoes

b)
1 a blue hat   3 a brown skirt
2 a green top   4 red boots

c)
1 a red dress   2 black shoes

d)
1 a grey suit   3 a white shirt
2 an orange tie   4 black and white trainers

2.36

Jasmine is wearing a red dress and black shoes.
Kate is wearing a blue hat, a green top, a brown skirt and red boots.
Jason is wearing a grey suit, an orange tie, a white shirt and black and white trainers.
Leon is wearing a black jacket, a yellow T-shirt, blue trousers and black shoes.

2.38

a) 'Are Lola and Ana wearing blue skirts?'
'Yes, they are.' 'No, they aren't.'
b) 'Are they dancing?'
'Yes, they are.' 'No, they aren't.'
c) 'Is Paolo wearing a uniform?'
'Yes, he is.' 'No, he isn't.'
d) 'Are Paolo and Elisa having a great time?'
'Yes, they are.' 'No, they aren't.'
e) 'Is Yuko wearing jeans?'
'Yes, she is.' 'No, she isn't.'
f) 'Is she holding a parasol?'
'Yes, she is.' 'No, she isn't.'

2.40

a) (H = Husband; W = Wife)
H: Hello, Kate.
W: Oh, hello, darling.
H: Where are you?
W: Oh, um, I'm in a shop.
H: What are you doing?
W: I'm buying fish for dinner.

b) (L = Liz; D = Don)
L: Hello, Don.
D: Oh, hi, Liz.
L: What are you doing?
D: I'm making dinner.
L: Ah, good.

c) (M = Mother; S = Son)
M: Hello.
S: Hi, Mum.
M: What are you doing?
S: I'm doing my homework.
M: Good boy.

2.41

a) do the housework, do the washing
b) make a coffee, make a phone call
c) play football, play the piano
d) read a book, read an email

Unit 11

2.45

a) the tenth of May
b) the eighteenth of June
c) the fifth of August
d) the sixteenth of August
e) the twenty-second of September
f) the fourteenth of November

2.46

a) 3 nineteen sixty-nine
b) 5 nineteen seventy-five
c) 2 nineteen eighty-nine
d) 6 nineteen ninety-seven
e) 1 two thousand and five
f) 4 two thousand and six

2.48

a) Welcome to *Spectacular Television Events*. Our first event is an important football match. On 9th July 2006, Italy won the World Cup in Germany. Three and a half billion people watched the match on television. France lost the match on penalties.

b) Our next event is Live 8. On 2nd July 2005, three billion people watched the Live 8 concerts on television. Paul McCartney, U2, Stevie Wonder, Björk and Coldplay were some of the big names at Live 8 concerts around the world.

c) The death of Princess Diana was a tragic event. On 6th September 1997, two and a half billion people watched her funeral on television. Prince William was fifteen years old, and Prince Harry was only twelve.

d) And finally, were you born when the first man landed on the Moon? On 20th July 1969 Neil Armstrong said the famous words, 'That's one small step for man, but one giant leap for mankind.' Five hundred million people watched the historic event on television.

2.49

a) 'Were you at secondary school in 2002?'
   'Yes, I was.' 'No, I wasn't.'
b) 'Were you at work yesterday?'
   'Yes, I was.' 'No, I wasn't.'
c) 'Was it sunny yesterday?'
   'Yes, it was.' 'No, it wasn't.'
d) 'Was your mother born before 1963?'
   'Yes, she was.' 'No, she wasn't.'
e) 'Were you and your friends in town yesterday?'
   'Yes, we were.' 'No, we weren't.'
f) 'Were your parents at university in 1975?'
   'Yes, they were.' 'No, they weren't.'

2.51

a) Japanese people were very excited.
b) In Paris the musicians weren't French!
c) It wasn't cold in Rome.
d) Brian Wilson was fantastic.
e) Elton John was terrible.
f) The political message was important.

2.52

(A = Andy; C = Cathy)
A: It was amazing!
C: It was awful!
C: It was boring!
A: It was excellent!
A: It was fantastic!
A: It was great!
C: It was terrible!
A: It was wonderful!

2.53

a) In Tokyo, the concert was amazing.
b) In Paris, the concert was awful.
c) In Rome, the music was excellent.
d) In Berlin, the bands were great.
e) In London, the concert was wonderful.
f) In Philadelphia, the concert was fantastic.

2.55

A: excellent, terrible, wonderful
B: amazing, delicious, expensive, fantastic, important

Unit 12

2.59

play basketball, go cycling, play football, play golf, go sailing, play tennis

2.61

a) He was born in 1971.
b) He got his first bicycle in 1978.
c) He graduated from high school in 1988.
d) He became a professional cyclist in 1992.
e) He had cancer in 1996.
f) He got married in 1997.
g) He started racing again in 1998.
h) He won the Tour de France for the seventh time in 2005.

2.62

a) He liked swimming and running when he was a child.
b) He joined the US Olympic team in 1988.
c) He finished last in his first important professional race.
d) He recovered from cancer after two operations and chemotherapy.
e) He started a cancer foundation in 1997.
f) He retired in 2005.

2.63

a) I used a computer.
b) I walked to work.
c) I planned a holiday.
d) I listened to music.
e) I cooked the dinner.
f) I studied English.

2.65

A: ask – asked, join – joined, pass – passed, play – played, watch – watched
B: hate – hated, point – pointed, want – wanted

2.67

Juan Sebastián Elcano was a Spanish explorer. He was born in 1476 in the north of Spain. In 1522 he completed the first voyage round the world.

In 1519 the king of Spain sent an expedition to find a route to the East. Ferdinand Magellan was the leader of the expedition, and he asked Elcano to go with him. They sailed from Spain with five ships.

Magellan died in the Philippines, but Elcano continued the voyage. In 1522 only one ship arrived back in Spain. 270 men started the voyage in 1519, but only 18 men returned.

2.68

(I = Interviewer; P = Pat; E = Eva; C = Carla)
1 I: Who's your hero in history?
   P: Mother Teresa.
   I: Why?
   P: Because she lived a very simple life and she gave all her time and her love to poor people.

2 I: Who's your hero in history?
   E: Beethoven.
   I: Why?
   E: Because he went deaf, but he wrote wonderful music.

3 I: Who's your hero in history?
   C: Leonardo da Vinci.
   I: Why?
   C: Because he was a genius. He did so many different things. He painted the Mona Lisa and he designed the first helicopter. Also, he was a vegetarian and he loved animals.

2.69

1 f 30 today! Happy birthday!
2 c It's a boy! Congratulations!
3 b Good luck in your exam!
4 e Happy 25th anniversary!
5 d Good luck in your new job!
6 a Happy New Year!

Review D

🎵 **2.72**

A: cheque, helped, jeans
B: football, jacket, started
C: audience, basketball, yesterday
D: amazing, fantastic, September

🎵 **2.74**

I was born in a little house in a village near Dublin. It was a very small house – very small – and I had ten brothers and sisters. My father was a farmer, and life was hard. My parents were very poor – they had no money. When I was seven I went to school in the village. There was one class and one teacher – Mr O'Sullivan. He was great! I loved school and I loved books. I wanted to go to university and become a doctor. But then when I graduated from school, I started work on the farm. I was sixteen. I got married when I was twenty. My husband, Cyril, was twenty-five.

Unit 13

🎵 **3.03**

Robin Knox-Johnston went round the world by boat. He travelled 48,197 kilometres. The journey took 312 days and one hour. He started the journey on 14th June 1968 and finished on 22nd April 1969.

🎵 **3.05**

Ewan McGregor and Charlie Boorman went round the world by motorbike. They travelled 30,395 kilometres. It took three and a half months. They started the journey on 14th April 2004 and finished on 29th July 2004.

🎵 **3.06**

a) 'Did they go round the world by motorbike?'
   'Yes, they did.' 'No, they didn't.'
b) 'Did they leave London on 14th May 2004?'
   'Yes, they did.' 'No, they didn't.'
c) 'Did they travel by car in Siberia?'
   'Yes, they did.' 'No, they didn't.'
d) 'Did they arrive in New York on 29th July 2004?'
   'Yes, they did.' 'No, they didn't.'
e) 'Did they meet a lot of children?'
   'Yes, they did.' 'No, they didn't.'
f) 'Did they sell their motorbikes?'
   'Yes, they did.' 'No, they didn't.'

🎵 **3.09 and 3.10**

(A = Alice; B = Ben)
A: Where did you go?
B: To Ibiza.
A: Why did you go there?
B: Because the hotel was cheap.
A: When did you go?
B: In July.
A: Who did you go with?
B: Will and Harry.
A: How did you travel?
B: By air.
A: What did you do?
B: We swam and went clubbing.

🎵 **3.11**

My best holiday was in the Maldives. It was last year, in December. I went with five friends. We went by air from London to Colombo in Sri Lanka and then to the Maldives. We stayed in a house near the beach. We went to the beach every day and one day we went swimming with sharks. That was amazing. We stayed for two weeks and we had a great time.

Unit 14

🎵 **3.15**

a) 'Can Nell Gifford perform on a horse?'
   'Yes, she can.' 'No, she can't.'
b) 'Can Gerald do circus tricks?'
   'Yes, he can.' 'No, he can't.'
c) 'Can Nancy dance and sing?'
   'Yes, she can.' 'No, she can't.'
d) 'Can the Kenyan Boys do acrobatics?'
   'Yes, they can.' 'No, they can't.'
e) 'Can Oleg lift 150 kilogrammes?'
   'Yes, he can.' 'No, he can't.'

🎵 **3.16**

a) Cats can see in the dark.
b) Lions can't run long distances.
c) Horses can sleep on their feet.
d) Lions can swim.
e) Horses can see colours.
f) Elephants can't jump.

🎵 **3.17**

a) Jim can swim.
b) Lance can't dance.
c) Clive can drive.
d) Lee can ski.
e) Dell can't spell.
f) Dwight can't write.

🎵 **3.18**

a) How many players are there in a basketball team?
b) How many letters are there in the English alphabet?
c) How many strings are there on a violin?
d) How many days are there in September?
e) How many states are there in the USA?
f) How many sports are there in a decathlon?

🎵 **3.19**

a) There are five players in a basketball team.
b) There are twenty-six letters in the English alphabet.
c) There are four strings on a violin.
d) There are thirty days in September.
e) There are fifty states in the USA.
f) There are ten sports in a decathlon.

🎵 **3.21**

Touch your head.
Touch your mouth.
Touch your nose.
Touch your back.
Touch your stomach.
Touch a tooth.
Touch your left ear.
Touch your right eye.
Touch your left arm.
Touch your right foot.
Touch your left leg.
Clap your hands!

Unit 15

🎵 **3.25**

a) 'Do you like cold weather?'
   'Yes I do.' 'No I don't.'
   'Would you like to visit Iceland?'
   'Yes I would.' 'No I wouldn't.'
b) 'Do you like extreme sports?'
   'Yes I do.' 'No I don't.'
   'Would you like to do a bungee jump?'
   'Yes I would.' 'No I wouldn't.'
c) 'Do you like fast cars?'
   'Yes I do.' 'No I don't.'
   'Would you like to drive a Ferrari?'
   'Yes I would.' 'No I wouldn't.'
d) 'Do you like Shakespeare?'
   'Yes I do.' 'No I don't.'
   'Would you like to see *Hamlet* at the Globe theatre in London?'
   'Yes I would.' 'No I wouldn't.'
e) 'Do you like the British Royal family?'
   'Yes I do.' 'No I don't.'
   'Would you like to meet the Queen?'
   'Yes I would.' 'No I wouldn't.'
f) 'Do you like travelling?'
   'Yes I do.' 'No I don't.'
   'Would you like to go round the world?'
   'Yes I would.' 'No I wouldn't.'

🎵 **3.26**

a) I'd like to go to the Moon.
b) My mother likes driving.
c) I wouldn't like to be famous.
d) My father doesn't like wine.
e) I'd like to learn to dance salsa.
f) I'd like to live in Canada.

🎵 **3.29**

a) 'Are you going to go shopping?'
   'Yes, I am.' 'No, I'm not.'
b) 'Are you going to meet a friend?'
   'Yes, I am.' 'No, I'm not.'
c) 'Are you going to drive home?'
   'Yes, I am.' 'No, I'm not.'
d) 'Are you going to go back to work?'
   'Yes, I am.' 'No, I'm not.'
e) 'Are you going to phone your friends?'
   'Yes, I am.' 'No, I'm not.'
f) 'Are you going to have a coffee?'
   'Yes, I am.' 'No, I'm not.'

🔊 **3.31**

B Who are you going to see?
  When are you going to see them?
  Why are you going to see them?
  What are they going to say?

C Who are you going to meet?
  When are you going to meet her?
  Why are you going to meet her?
  What's she going to say?

🔊 **3.32**

(I = Interviewer; J = Justin; K = Kelly)
I: Congratulations! You won €10 million.
    How are you going to celebrate?
J: Oh, we're going to have a big party
    with all our friends.
K: No, no, we're not going to have a big
    party. We're going to have a quiet party
    with our family. And then we're going
    to go on holiday.
I: Where are you going to go?
K: To India.
J: To America.
K: I want to see the Taj Mahal.
J: And I want to see the Grand Canyon.
I: Um, are you going to buy a new house?
K: Yes, we're going to buy a house
    in Spain.
J: France. We're going to buy a house
    in France.
K: Spain.
I: And are you going to give some money
    to your family?
K: Yes. We're going to buy a new car for
    my mother.
J: A new car for your mother? I want
    a new car.
I: Do you think you're going to be
    happy?
K: Oh yes! Of course.
J: Hmm!

🔊 **3.36**

(M = Man; W = Woman)
a) W: How much are these?
   M: Twenty euros.
b) W: This is John.
   M: Nice to meet you.
c) M: Can I speak to Mr Brown, please?
   W: I'm sorry. He's out.
d) W: What time is it in London?
   M: It's 9.30 in the morning.
e) M: Excuse me. Is there a bank near
       here?
   W: Er, yes – over there.
f) M: Would you like a cup of tea?
   W: No, thanks.
g) M: Can I have a cappuccino, please?
   W: Small, medium or large?
h) W: Can I help you?
   M: Yes, I'm looking for a tie.
i) W: It's my English exam today.
   M: Oh, good luck!
j) M: What's the matter?
   W: I have toothache.

Review E

🔊 **3.37**

A: birthday, journey, mountain, weather
B: bicycle, dangerous, holiday, nobody
C: ago, arrive, hotel, perform

🔊 **3.39**

(D = Darren; A = Amy)
D: I have Amy from White Nights here in
    the studio. Amy, welcome.
A: Thanks. It's good to be here.
D: How long are you going to stay in
    New Zealand?
A: We're going to stay for six days.
D: Great! Where are you going to go after
    New Zealand?
A: We're going to go to Australia. We have
    two concerts in Sydney.
D: Ah. When did you start the tour?
A: We started four weeks ago – on
    22nd December.
D: Four weeks ago? I see. How do you
    usually travel?
A: Usually by plane. We sometimes travel
    by car on very short journeys, but we
    usually go by plane.
D: What do you all like doing when
    you're not working?
A: Well, Baz likes sightseeing – and he
    loves museums. Olly likes all sports, so
    he usually tries to find somewhere to
    swim or play football. Tom and I like
    shopping, and that's where we spend
    all of our time and money.
D: Thank you very much for coming in,
    Amy. I hope you have a good time here
    in New Zealand, and please come back
    soon.
A: Thank you very much.

Phonetic symbols

Single vowels

/ɪ/	fish	/fɪʃ/
/iː/	bean	/biːn/
/ʊ/	foot	/fʊt/
/uː/	shoe	/ʃuː/
/e/	egg	/eg/
/ə/	mother	/ˈmʌðə/
/ɜː/	word	/wɜːd/
/ɔː/	talk	/tɔːk/
/æ/	back	/bæk/
/ʌ/	bus	/bʌs/
/ɑː/	arm	/ɑːm/
/ɒ/	top	/tɒp/

Diphthongs

/ɪə/	ear	/ɪə/
/eɪ/	face	/feɪs/
/ʊə/	tourist	/ˈtʊərɪst/
/ɔɪ/	boy	/bɔɪ/
/əʊ/	nose	/nəʊz/
/eə/	hair	/heə/
/aɪ/	eye	/aɪ/
/aʊ/	mouth	/maʊθ/

Consonants

/p/	pen	/pen/
/b/	bag	/bæg/
/t/	tea	/tiː/
/d/	dog	/dɒg/
/tʃ/	chip	/tʃɪp/
/dʒ/	jazz	/dʒæz/
/k/	cake	/keɪk/
/g/	girl	/gɜːl/
/f/	film	/fɪlm/
/v/	verb	/vɜːb/
/θ/	thing	/θɪŋ/
/ð/	these	/ðiːz/
/s/	snake	/sneɪk/
/z/	zoo	/zuː/
/ʃ/	shop	/ʃɒp/
/ʒ/	television	/ˈtelɪvɪʒən/
/m/	map	/mæp/
/n/	name	/neɪm/
/ŋ/	ring	/rɪŋ/
/h/	house	/haʊs/
/l/	leg	/leg/
/r/	road	/rəʊd/
/w/	wine	/waɪn/
/j/	yes	/jes/

Stress

Word stress is shown by underlining the stressed syllable:
water, amazing, Japanese.

Letters of the alphabet

/eɪ/	/iː/	/e/	/aɪ/	/əʊ/	/uː/	/ɑː/
Aa	Bb	Ff	Ii	Oo	Qq	Rr
Hh	Cc	Ll	Yy		Uu	
Jj	Dd	Mm			Ww	
Kk	Ee	Nn				
	Gg	Ss				
	Pp	Xx				
	Tt	Zz				
	Vv					

Irregular verbs

Infinitive	Past simple
be	was / were
become	became
begin	began
break	broke
bring	brought /brɔːt/
buy	bought /bɔːt/
can	could /kʊd/
choose	chose
come	came
cost	cost
do	did
draw	drew
drink	drank
drive	drove
eat	ate
fall	fell
feel	felt
find	found
forget	forgot
get	got
give	gave
go	went
have	had
hear	heard /hɜːd/
hold	held
keep	kept
know	knew /njuː/
leave	left
lose	lost
make	made
mean	meant /ment/
meet	met
pay	paid
put	put
read	read /red/
ride	rode
ring	rang
run	ran
say	said /sed/
see	saw /sɔː/
sell	sold
send	sent
sit	sat
sleep	slept
speak	spoke
spend	spent
stand	stood
swim	swam
take	took /tʊk/
teach	taught /tɔːt/
tell	told
think	thought /θɔːt/
understand	understood
wake	woke
wear	wore /wɔː/
win	won /wʌn/
write	wrote

Macmillan Education
Between Towns Road, Oxford OX4 3PP
A division of Macmillan Publishers Limited
Companies and representatives throughout the world

ISBN 978-1-4050-7055-3

First published 2007

Review units by Peter Maggs and Catherine Smith
Project management by Desmond O'Sullivan, Quality Outcomes Limited
Designed by 320 Design Limited
Photographic research and editorial by Sally Cole, Perseverance Works Limited
Illustrated by Beach pp8, 11, 15, 23, 33, 34, 39, 42, 45, 46, 47, 55, 61, 67, 77, 83,
85, 89, 94, 99, 105, 111, 113r; Luisa Jones p18; Ed McLachlan pp10, 16, 22, 24, 32,
38, 44, 54, 59, 60, 66, 74, 75, 76, 82, 88, 90, 91, 96, 98, 104, 107, 108, 110, 112,
113l, 117, 122, 127, 128, 133, 135; Tobatron pp56, 57; Adrian Valencia pp119, 124;
Kim Williams pp13, 40, 51
Cover design by Andrew Oliver

Authors acknowledgements
We would like to thank all our students and colleagues at the Oxford English Centre
in Oxford. In particular Graham Simpson, Meriel Steele, John Fitch and Colin
Lockhart who made it possible for us to continue teaching beginner level classes
throughout the time we were writing. Your help has been invaluable.
We would also like to thank our teacher colleagues around the world who are using
Inside Out – your feedback has confirmed that we're doing something right, and
helped us identify what we should keep and what we could improve. Particular
thanks go to Spanish EOI teachers, Vicki Samaniego, Fernando Martín, Fernando Alba
and José María Mateo for their helpful reports. Other teachers and institutions we
would like to thank include: Anthony Sheridan (British Council, Bangkok), Michael
Wiener (Siam Computer, Bangkok), Carole Hughes and Russ Evans (British Council,
Chiang Mai); Maya Neishtadt, Yana Orlitskaya, Svetlana Babaeva, Professor Tatiana
Shepelenk, Natalia Potapova, Suriya Shukurova, Irina Kruglova, Gillian Davidson,
Madina Fiodorova, Professor Olga Kolykhalova, Natalia Kolesnikova and Professor Olga
Kaznina (Moscow); Peter Tamkin and Phil Hopkins (English Language Centre,
Brighton); as well as the staff and students at Oxford House College (London),
St Giles College (London), EF (London), Aspect ILA (London), Regent School (London),
Wimbledon School of English (London) and Francis King School of English (London).
We are especially grateful to Peter Maggs and Catherine Smith for the wonderful
New Inside Out Workbook as well as their Student's Book review units, and to Helena
Gomm, Caroline Brown, David Seymour and Chris Dawson for their important
contributions to the New Inside Out Teacher's Book.
At Macmillan Education, we would like to thank Kate Melliss, Rafael Alarcon-Gaeta,
Karen White, Balvir Koura, Bryan Fletcher, Jemma Harrison, Guy Jackson and
Stephanie Parker.
We would also like to thank Sally Cole (freelance photo researcher), Alyson Maskell,
Celia Bingham and Xanthe Sturt Taylor (freelance editors) and James Richardson
(freelance audio producer).
Jackie Hill and Kim Williams – our wonderfully talented freelance designers – deserve
several medals for their hard work and dedication, and for regularly going the extra
mile. Inside Out would not be the stylish course it is without them, or without
Andrew Oliver's fabulous cover design. We should probably thank Mark Rothko for his
contribution too.
Many thanks also go to the Macmillan production and marketing teams, and in
particular Jo Greig whose enthusiasm and encouragement have been such a support.
We reserve our biggest thanks for Des O'Sullivan (freelance project manager). It's
great to be working with you again, Des – always a privilege – and as usual the
project has benefited from your humour, sensitivity, drive and sheer professionalism.
We consider ourselves very fortunate to be working with someone who is so very
obviously at the top of their profession. Thanks, Des.
Finally, we are so grateful to our families for their ongoing support and
understanding. In particular Sue would like to thank her mum and dad. Even though
it hasn't been a great year for you, you have continued to give me 100% unconditional
support and encouragement. You have no idea how important that is to me.
This book is dedicated to Sue Bale and David Riley – our heartfelt thanks go to you
for your inspirational contribution to the Inside Out series, and your constant
support over the years.

The authors and publishers would like to thank the following for permission to
reproduce their photographs: Action Plus/C.Villa p14(d), S.Bardens p79(c);
Alamy/onrequest images p12(2), W.Diggles p19(a), R.Kelly p24(a), A.Jenny p24(c),
Scenics & Science p24(e), eye35.com p26(rb), A room with views p26(rm),
Maximilian p28(fruit), A.Proust p28(wine), I.Townsley p28(coffee), foodfolio
p28(Italian), T.Hill p28(meat), A.Segre p30(3), Travelstock44 p 30(4), P.Tweedie
p36(a), R.Naude pp36(b), 122(c), B.Bachman p36(d), D.Hancock p36(ba), PCL
p52(2), A.Segre p52(4), R.Levine p54(a), Culliganphoto p54(c), B.Lyons p58(3),
K.Miyoshi p58(2), profimedia p58(1), T.Klassen p65, R.Harding p69(1), BL Images
pp69(2), (5), D.Sanger p69(3), M.Kipling p69(4), R.Fried p69(8), D.Noton p69(9),
A.von Einsiedel p70(bl), S.Cordaiy Photolibrary p70(bm), C.Ehlers p71(tl), BL Images
p71(b), P.Cook p71(tm), F.Chmura p73(1), K.Welsh p73(3), J.Smith p80(br), J.Hart
p93(t), Photolibrary Wales p93(mt), W. Diggles pp93(m), 116(bm), L.Dwight
p93(mb), A.Rohmer p93(b), D. Smith p93(l), Arco Images p102(tr), C.McLennan
p115(b), Eye35.com p115(m), Stock Connection Distribution p116(bl), Bubbles
Photolibrary p116(br), Photofusion/C.Edwards p121(mb), J.Kase p121(br), P.Titmuss
p129; Collections/O.Benn p26(rt); Corbis/MGM p6(t), Sygma p6(b), Lucidio Studio
inc p12(1), C.Schneider p12(3), LWA-S.Kennedy pp12(6), 13(t), R.Folkks p14(a),
G.Gramann/Zefa p19(b), P.Giardino p21(t), D.Modricker p21(b), T.Stewart
p28(football), Photocuisine p28(tea), Free Agents Ltd p 31, W.Stone p36(e),
LWA/D.Tardif p36(bb), 122(a), Virgo p36(be), 117(a), F.Vogt p37(4), E.Holub p43,
Newmann p48(b), S.Pitamitz p49, B.Zaunders p50(3), L.Lefkowitz p50(4), B.Krist
p50(5), A.Schein pp50(6), (7), M. Yamashita p52(5), R.Folkks p56(r). T.Manske
p70(br), F.Frei p71(tr), B.S.P.I. p73(2), F.Trapper p78(b), Reuters pp78(e), 87(b),
B.Bird p81(b), Bettmann p84(b), A.Bianchi p84(c), O. Hoslet p85(bl), S. Bianchetti
p87(a), A.Iconografico p87(c), S.Pitamitz p97, P.Souders p101(r), J.Koenig p102(bl),
A di Meo/Ansa/EPA p106(5), W.Manning p106(8), K.Ruge p114(l), K.Mitchell
p114(ml), Grace p114(mr), SIE Productions p114(r), M. Powell p115(t),
S.Cardinale/Peoples Avenue pp116(2). 121(2), M.Hartmann pp116(3), 121(3),
J.Henley p121(bl); Empics/P.Jordan p42, D.Mills p78(c), M.Fearn p78(f), I.West/PA
p80(l), ABACA Press pp84(a), p116(b), 121(b); Getty Images/P. Dazeley p12(4), DK
Stock pp12(5), 13(b), G.Hellier p14(e), M.Newman p17(1), Y.Tsuno p24(d),
S.Wilkinson p28(swimmer), S.Forster p28(tennis), K.Arras p28(Chinese), Picturepress
p29(t), W.Walton p30(2), J.Cummins p36(c). 117(c), J.Share p36(f), S.Justice
p36(bc), B.Thomas pp36(bd), 122(b), Yellow Dog Productions p37(1), D.Vervitis
p37(2), F.Lucano p37(3), AB p37(5), H.Neleman p40, G.Faint p50(2), D.Johns
p52(apple), M.Tama p54(b), S.Chernin p54(d), Hulton Archive pp56(l), 92(r), P.Hince
p58(a), M.Prince p58(b), D.Sacks p58(c), R.Meinychuk p58(5), A.Caulfield p58(6),
J.Cornish p69(6), D.Endersbee p69(7), J.Kirn p70(t), Digital Vision RF p70(m),
F.Calfat p72(a), F.Harrison p72(b), C.Jackson p72(c), P.Riviere p72(d), M.Kim p78(a),
J.McHugh p79(a), Muntz p80(tl), S.Hald p80(mtl), C.Wilhelm p80(bml), S.Cohen
p80(tr), D.Vervits p80(bl), D.Robcis p80(mtr), L.Bobbe p80(mbr), M.Mochet p84(d),
P.Andrieu p85(l), F. Vogel p85(tl), T.Morrison p92(l), S.Justice p93(mb), B.Stefko
p(tr), J.Martin p101(m), M.Bartley p102(tl), M.Nichols p102(tm), K.Tirkkonen
p102(br), Kofujiwara p106(1), p106(6), E.Dryer p106(9), S.Studd p16(10), B.Martin
pp109(t), p109(b), M.Cardy p114(b), S.Gries p116(1), 121(1), B.Bedder pp116(4),
121(4), F.Harrison p116(5), 119(c), 121(5), 124(c), D.Hogan p116(6), 121(6),
C.Alvarez pp116(a), 121(a), D.Feingold p116(b), 121(b), E.Agostini p116(e),
121(e), S.Finn p116(f), 121(f), D.Westing p119(a), 124(a), P.Le Segretain
pp119(d), 124(d); Guinness World Records p94(b); Kobal/Danjaq/Eon/UA/
K.Hamshere p7; NASA Images p107; National Trust Picture Library/R.Thrift p56(ml),
D.Gilbert p57(tl).(tr), (b); NHPA/Y.Lanceau p101(l); Photolibrary/C.Abad p28(coke),
Foodpix p28(fish), Cwener Photography p34, Onrequest Images p41, E.Davies p50(1),
A.Butera p52(1), D.Carrasco p52(3), Y.Cardozo p53, G.Hellier p58(4), Alder p106(2),
R.Gloria p106(4), Reso E.E.I.D p118; Photolibrary Wales p26(l); PPL Photo Agency
p94(t); Rex Features pp14(c), 20, 87(l), 106(3), E.Vidal p14(b), T.Jockmans p14(f),
F.Dean p14(f), P.Brooker p20(2), Charbonneau/Bei p36(bf), 117(b), R.Schwanke
p56(mr), Sipa Press pp79(d), 85(ml), M.Hardie pp116(c), 119(b), 121(c), 124(b),
SAE/Keystone USA pp116(d), 121(d); Topfoto/J.Turner p78(d), UPP p79(c), Pro Sport
pp84(e),(f); Wenn p20(1); Macmillan/Bananastock pp15, 17(4), 17(5), 25, 86, 81(t),
Image Source p17(2), 17(3), Brand X p17(6), Corbis rf p17 (7), 17(8);
Photodisc p21.
Photographs on pp18, 19(c), published with kind permission of Vaughan Jones; Nina
Frank p29(b), published with kind permission of Sue Kay; Giffords Circus photographs
on p100, published with kind permission of James Waddell and Giffords Circus;
Photograph of Dan Hovey on p48, published with kind permission of Dan Hovey;
Photographs on page 64 all kindly supplied by Mike Pugh; Ewan McGregor and
Charlie Boorman published with kind permission of The Long Way Round p95.
Commissioned photography by Chris King pp4, 5, 8, 26, 27, 62, 63. Dean Ryan
pp9, 51.

Printed and bound in Spain by Edelvives

2011 2010 2009 2008 2007
10 9 8 7 6 5 4 3 2

07/1930/ 25
16·87